HERBERT AUSTIN'S HEAVY TWELVE-FOUR 1922-39

JIM STRINGER

Herridge & Sons

MICHAEL SEDGWICK
MEMORIAL TRUST

Herbert Austin's Heavy Twelve-Four is published with the financial assistance of the Michael Sedgwick Memorial Trust. The M.S.M.T. was founded in memory of the motoring historian and author Michael C. Sedgwick (1926–1983) to encourage the publication of new motoring research, and the recording of Road Transport History. Support by the Trust does not imply any involvement in the editorial process, which remains the responsibility of the editor and publisher. The Trust is a Registered Charity, No 290841, and a full list of the Trustees and an overview of the functions of the M.S.M.T. can be found on: www.michaelsedgwicktrust.co.uk

Published in 2021 By
Herridge & Sons Ltd
Lower Forda, Shebbear
Beaworthy, Devon EX21 5SY

© Copyright James Stringer 2021

Design: Chris Fayers

All rights reserved. No part of this publication may be reproduced in any form or by any means without the prior written permission of the publisher and the copyright holder.

ISBN 978-1-914929-00-7
Printed in China

Contents

Chapter 1:	History and technical description of the Austin Twelve	9
Chapter 2:	The motoring press and the Austin Twelve	22
Chapter 3:	How they were made	36
Chapter 4:	The standard factory body styles	40
Chapter 5:	Special and special-bodied cars, at home and abroad	54
Chapter 6:	And they were raced too!	68
Chapter 7:	Brochures, advertising, and publicity	73
Chapter 8:	The Twelve as a workhorse: The Taxi story in peace and war	85
Chapter 9:	Stories from owners, in fact – and in fiction	102
Chapter 10:	Survivors and losers: Twelves adapted, reborn, or destroyed	109
Appendix	Car numbers, change points, prices, and production figures	119

Dedication

I dedicate this book to the memory of the late Robert (Bob) Wyatt, MBE, who I genuinely believe was responsible for the fact that so many Austin Twelve-Fours have survived to this day.

It was back in the mid-1950s, when the value of thirty-to-forty year old motor cars was at their lowest and they were therefore more likely to be scrapped in favour of newer models, that Bob took the initiative to form a club, The Vintage Austin Twelve-Four Register, where owners could come together and focus on keeping these cars on the road.

Today, a century on since the first Austin Twelve was sold, there are known to be several thousand of them still providing pleasurable motoring for dedicated owners in many countries around the world. This book is therefore not only a tribute to the car itself, but to the man who cared and catered for their survival.

Foreword
by the late Michael Worthington-Williams MBE

Mike Worthington-Williams MBE

Having owned an Austin Seven box saloon, a 20/4 Carlton saloon and three of the later Austin Somersets, I feel that I am justified in saying that I am an Austin man. I would add that I have covered 40,000 trouble free miles in a Seven, moved house twice in it, and was stopped by the police in it on the A20. "Why are you driving so slowly sir, have you been drinking?" "No officer, I'm moving house. I have a wheelbarrow, a fridge and a gate-legged table in here with me, and I can't get out of second gear!" Those wide doors were a godsend!

I used the 20/4 as everyday wheels for twenty-five years, clocking up a quarter of a million miles, both in the UK, the Republic of Ireland and in France, and never came home on the end of a rope. The Somersets all also gave good, reliable service, with separate chassis frames and robustly built bodywork. But I have never owned a Heavy 12/4 – the subject of this book.

I am, however, very familiar with them, having been associated with Sotheby's, Brooks and Bonhams auction houses for the last forty years as a consultant. During that time I have driven many Twelves, and can well understand their reputation for near-indestructibility and reliability. Up until now there has been no in-depth book about this most worthy of cars, which epitomised Herbert Austin's philosophy that his cars must demonstrate longevity, robust construction and sound engineering, and represent good value for money.

No one is more qualified to write this book than Jim Stringer. I doubt if any living person knows more about the Austin Heavy 12/4 than him.

Here we have the history behind the model's introduction, contemporary press reports, early advertisements, and from the first brochure issued up until 1934-35 the various body styles available. Those which were exported as chassis to New Zealand and Australia and then bodied locally are also included. The taxicabs have a section to themselves, as does the different coachwork available from various coachbuilders – including the work they undertook during the war.

When many cabs dating from the thirties were pensioned off in the early fifties, they took on many other roles, and Jim details some of them. Separate chapters are reserved for 12/4s which have earned their own special place in the Austin Twelve's history; these include "Peggy", the cab featured in the film *Carry on Cabby*, and "Gumdrop", the tourer immortalised by the late Val Biro.

The Austin 12/4 has survived in respectable numbers, and if you are wondering why, Jim's book will leave you in no doubt. Everything you need to know about the Heavy 12/4 Austin, including contemporary road tests and stories of restorations, is in this book. In 2022 we celebrate the centenary of the addition of this model to the Austin range, and it is most appropriate that this comprehensive tribute should be published to coincide with this. I feel privileged to have been asked to write this foreword.

Author's note: Sadly Mike passed away at the age of 83 in February 2021 while this book was in preparation.

Author's introduction

My first Austin was in fact a 1935 10hp Lichfield saloon given to me by my local vicar, who had replaced it with an early 1950s Ford Prefect. However, the 10/4 was a non-runner and it had to be pushed from the vicar's garage to the one attached to my parent's house in Acton, West London. I was not old enough to drive at that time, but was happy to "tinker" with this car in order to gain some experience for when the day came for me to become a fully-fledged motorist. In truth I never succeeded in getting the car going and sadly it went to the scrapyard, for which I received thirty bob (£1.50).

It was whilst taking driving lessons a year or so later that I noticed a very old Austin parked under a tree looking a bit the worse for wear. But there was something about this old car which made me want to own it. I mentioned this to my driving instructor who thought I was crazy to even consider owning a thing like that, after all, I was taking my driving lessons in a new Triumph Herald. This was in 1962.

The owner of the Austin was, as it so happened, quite willing to sell me the car, which turned out to be a 1929 six-cylinder 16 horsepower fabric-bodied saloon, for the princely sum of £50, but as I did not have that amount of money, we haggled and I eventually paid just £35 for it, and, believe it or not, I still have that car today!

My next step was to join a club which would help me if I ever needed it, and that's when I became a member of the Vintage Austin Register. In the course of the past 58 years of membership, I have served on the committee in various roles including Honorary Secretary, Chairman and Editor of the Register's quarterly magazine for 17 years, after which I was made a Life Member and Vice President back in the late 1990s.

After my retirement from work, I was able to indulge in two ambitions. Writing, and conducting research into the history of the Austin Motor Company, and to these ends I have had four books published which are *An Austin Anthology* (volumes I, II & III), and *My Life with an Austin Sixteen-Six*.

The author's 1929 Austin Sixteen-Six fabric-bodied saloon.

Acknowledgements

In order to ensure that a book which sets out to be the definitive history of the Austin Twelve-Four covers every possible aspect of this quite remarkable motor car, I have been able to call upon many present-day owners for photographs and their experiences. I have also been very fortunate to be given access to a considerable amount of archive material held by individuals and Austin motor clubs, which have enhanced my own knowledge of Herbert Austin's Heavy Twelve-Four. But why "Heavy"? – This addition was due solely to the introduction in 1932 of the Austin Light 12/4 (of 11.9 rather than 12.8 RAC hp). In listing those who have very kindly provided me with such help and information. It is inevitable that I will have inadvertently omitted a few names from the list, for which I must apologise.

Clubs:
The Vintage Austin Register (VAR), The Ulster Pre-war Austin Club, The London Vintage Taxi Association, The Vintage Austin Registers of New Zealand and Australia, The Austin Club of Holland.

Individuals:
Barry Bain, John Bedford, Anthony Blackman, Ian Brough, David Cantor, Mr T Clarke, Anders Ditlev Clausager, Murray Cockburn, Barry Davies, Jim Dean, Mr D Dickinson, Michael Eggenton, Suzanne Finch, Michael Flack, Peter Fry, Cairns Fulton, Mike Gibson, James Gray, Brad Hallows, David Heatley, Bob Hughes, Jodi Kaldenberg, Robert Kendall, Keith Laidlow, Denis Le Cren, R Long, Mike Luff, Duncan Lye, George McGuire, Paul Martyn, Anthony Mealing, Alan Milliner, Dennis Milne, Neil Mosley, Peter Moyle, Brian Parker, Brian Porter, Stephen Postlethwaite, Mr M Rolls, Awini Ambuj Shanker, Anthony Smallbone, Gary Stringer, Bill Taylor, Chris Theakstone, Norman Tidd, Dr Damian Tominey, Barry Weatherhead, Michael Wheeler-Wyatt, Mr C Williams, Terry Wilson, the late Michael Worthington-Williams MBE, Peter Wright, and the late RJ "Bob" Wyatt MBE.

Further recommended reading:
An Austin Anthology (I) J Stringer
An Austin Anthology (II) J Stringer
An Austin Anthology (III) J Stringer.
My Life with an Austin Sixteen-Six J Stringer.
The Austin (Men & Motors) B Sharratt
Lord Austin – The Man RJ Wyatt and ZE Lambert (out of print)
The Austin 1905-1952 RJ Wyatt (out of print)
Taxicabs (A Photographic History) P Warren and Malcolm Linskey
London Taxis at War A Townsend
The London Taxi N Georgano
The Book of the Austin Twelve Garbutt & Twelvetrees

Chapter One

HISTORY AND TECHNICAL DESCRIPTION OF THE AUSTIN TWELVE-FOUR

This section was researched and written by the late Bob Wyatt MBE for *Old Motor* magazine back in the 1970s, and must, quite rightly, be considered to be the "Gold Standard" on the Austin Twelve and therefore an appropriate way in which to commence the history of this remarkable motor car. Bob's son, Michael, has kindly agreed to the inclusion of this article.

The usual difficulties experienced in getting production underway, coupled with the obvious cash-flow problems, no doubt swayed Herbert Austin to start the post-war production with one model, especially as his experience in war production had proved that cheapness and quantity production could result from a one-model policy.

The type of car which was doing best in 1913 was an owner-driven 20hp vehicle, of which Austin produced 983 in the last twelve months of peace, and the thinking in 1917 was that the production of such a vehicle would be the best solution when the war ended. By 1918, the scene was set for the Austin Twenty, a really excellent car, which could be built on mass-produced lines at what was then considered to be an economic price. The demand for cars during 1919 outstripped the supply, but the moulders' strike, galloping inflation, coupled with a serious shortage of steel and other raw materials, meant that Austin had to raise the price of the Twenty from £495 to £695 in the first year of production.

Only 543 20s were built in the twelve months from the recommencement of car production in July 1919, though the next two years were rather better, with 2246 sold in the first eleven months of 1920. A slump in trade followed in 1921 and by the end of the year it became almost impossible to sell enough cars or tractors based on the 20hp components to keep the factory at Longbridge running.

Front cover from 1922 catalogue.

Austin had become a public company in 1914, and their financial position had become so bad after the war that by 1921 a receiver was appointed. Herbert Austin's own wealth was also decimated and the story goes that on factory pay-days, he would cycle out of reach in the Lickey Hills until he heard that the wages money had been successfully raised. Fortunately, with the aid of fresh capital and the help of suppliers, the company managed to stay in business and indeed between 1926 and 1934 showed an average gross profit of over £1.1 million each year.

It became very obvious that the post-war motorists were now of a new breed. Thousands upon thousands of ex-servicemen who had been given the opportunity of learning to drive in the war came home determined to be car owners. The pre-war wealthy were now not so

Sir Herbert Austin in the prototype Austin Twelve.

wealthy and the large, hand-built cars, produced in their dozens, or at the most in their hundreds, were "out" in the new, radical post-war world. Austin was able to see the coming market opportunities and visualised scaled-down versions of the 20hp in 10hp and 5hp guises, thereby offering a car to cater for all pockets. The first of these to get underway became the 12/4 in 1921, followed in 1922 by the Seven.

Manufacture of a prototype 12/4 began in July 1921 and the car, albeit unfinished, was tested by a writer for a motoring weekly in September. To achieve the scoop, his test run was made at Longbridge in a bare chassis before the body was fitted. Two weeks later the car was complete and was reviewed by other journalists. It had a four-door, four-seater touring body and ran on unusual Michelin four-stud wheels fitted with 760x90 beaded-edge tyres [*on production cars, wood-spoke wheels were fitted and the tyre size was increased to 765x105mm*]. Compared to the Twenty, the track was reduced from 4ft 8in (1422mm) to 4ft (1219mm) and the engine from 3600cc to 1661cc; at that period, quite small by Austin standards. It weighed 16cwt (814kg) and was described by the factory a "car of moderate dimensions which would fulfil ideals of service previously only obtainable in high powered cars of 20hp and over".

After a test drive, one writer commented upon the top gear acceleration from 20mph (32 km/h), a noted feature of the flexible Austin Twelve engine which, with its five-bearing crankshaft, was always particularly smooth in top, and which lasted indefinitely. Many drivers found this feature important because it required a great deal of practice to manipulate the 12/4 gearbox. Once completely mastered, however, it was only necessary to use the clutch from a standstill, although no great top speeds were noted on the test runs – 45 to 47mph (72-76 km/h) and 50mph (80 km/h) "with modified carburettor" – fuel consumption was over 30mpg (9.4 litres per 100km). The smooth-running short-stroke four-cylinder monobloc engine with detachable head had a bore of 72mm and a stroke of 102mm, much shorter than was customary for a bore of that size in the early 1920s. This resulted in quite a high-revving unit for the period. Helped by the provision of aluminium pistons, and though the official RAC rating was 12.8hp, 20bhp was developed at 2000rpm.

By January 1922 three body styles were offered: the four-seater tourer at £550, a two-seater at £550 and a two-door coupé with four seats at £695, all models using twelve-spoke wooden wheels with 765mm x 105mm tyres. Another version of the Twelve, which remained in production until 1925, was a small version of the luxurious Sizaire-Berwick [*described in chapter 5 of this book*], whose manufacturers had been inexplicably acquired by Austin in 1923.

The very first Austin Twelve was sold through Carlaws, the Glasgow Austin dealership, in January 1922. Carlaws had exhibited the Twelve at the Scottish Motor Show, which was also held in January.

By September 1922 an effort had been made to increase sales. Since production had begun some nine months before, only 51 chassis, 809 tourers and 305 coupés had been sold, and to improve the situation two utility versions of the car were offered. The two-seater and four-seater tourers could be obtained, in one colour only, with a spare wheel without a tyre, at £450. The so-called "specials" cost £490 and included rear screens and the fifth tyre, and were obtainable in Elephant Grey, Royal Blue or Maroon. The coupé was given the name Harley and, provided with a leather hood, cost £600, the same price being charged for a landaulet, called the Berkeley. Although the 12 chassis was unaltered for the 1923 Motor Show, it now came with spring gaiters, clock, electric horn and luggage carrier. Production data for the period to 31 October 1923 does not show that any two-seaters were made at that time. None have survived to prove that they were, and if there were any the figure must have been very small.

All the early cars with the 4ft track were given the car number prefix T. Additional letters denoted the model throughout the period of Austin 12 production: TT for tourer, TC for saloon, TS for special body, and TF for fabric. With each major design change, a number prefixed the T. 2T, introduced in May 1923, related to an increase in track to 4ft 4in (1321mm); and with the increase the car was described as a five seater. The first cars were so narrow that the steering box had to be bolted to the outside of the chassis frame, which necessitated a slot being cut in the wing, covered by a shaped metal cowl. When the width was increased, there was enough room in the engine compartment to take the complete steering box, but it was not until August that this was done. [*This is a misunderstanding; the steering box was always inside the chassis, but on the early cars the drop arm was outside.*]

In November 1923 the Windsor saloon was first announced, and it is interesting to see how this style of body became increasingly popular at the expense of the open touring car. In 1924 550 saloons were made compared with 2950 tourers, by 1927 the saloon production had reached 5000 and the tourer 8000. By 1928 more saloons were made than open cars, and by 1930 there were more than three saloons to every tourer. By 1932 the Austin 12 open car had become a rarity.

In the early days, quite a high proportion of the 12/4 output was in chassis form, the chassis going to special body builders in some cases, but most of them being exported. The first special bodies were not announced until January 1924, when a two-three seater coupé body by Chalmer-Hoyer was advertised at £550 and a Gordon coupé at the same price.

October 1924 saw the next major change with the introduction of the 3T series, when the four-wheel brake system was adopted and friction dampers were attached to each spring. The system was very simple and avoided some of the more complicated front brake devices, and although the Twelve was never famous for its braking efficiency, at least the four-wheeled system was smooth in operation, and a distinct advantage over the puny rear wheel brakes. For the Motor Show in 1924, prices were revised and reduced considerably. The chassis cost £270, the Hertford and the five-seater tourer [*now for the first time bearing the name Clifton*] were £355, the Harley all-weather and the Berkeley landaulet, £475, with the Windsor saloon £425.

In 1925 the production rose to about 8450, more than twice the number built the previous year. There were no major changes in the specification of the 3T, landaulets and two-four seaters were made in only limited numbers and there were about 5400 tourers sold against 2500 Windsor saloons.

Standard body colours for 1924 and 1925 were Royal Blue, Kingfisher Blue, Elephant Grey, Brown and Maroon. Beaded-edge tyres were now fitted to ten-spoke Dunlop [*probably Sankey*] metal wheels. The track was still 4ft 4in, and the 6-volt electrical system used a narrow battery along the side of the exhaust silencer under the front passenger seat.

By now, cars were becoming faster and more powerful, and to remain competitive the engine of the 12/4 had to be increased in size. Before the introduction of the new model the 1926 prices were £245 for the chassis, £295 for the Clifton, £315 for the two-seater,

An Austin publicity photo showing a mid-1920s Clifton against the background of a half-timbered building.

£395 for the Windsor and £405 for the new Iver Saloon, which differed from the Windsor by the introduction of a division between the front and rear compartments, with a central rise-and-fall window. In each case these prices were about £50 more than the equivalent Morris Oxford, 11.9 Bean or 11.9 Clyno, though the fairer comparison is with cars of similar quality like the 12/35 Swift at £295 for the chassis and £375 for the tourer, or the 12/25 Humber at £350 to £440.

There was also a Mulliner-built saloon for £365, a Gordon saloon landaulet for £425 with the option of having a division fitted for an extra £10. Finally, the Chalmer-Hoyer three-seater coupé cost £450. All these models had 30in by 5in balloon tyres and 6-volt electrical systems. The new engine – known as the long-stroke engine – increased the bhp at 2000rpm to 27, by increasing the stroke to 114.5mm and the capacity from 1661cc to 1861cc; this did not raise the RAC hp which was based on the bore size only, upon which the motor tax rates were calculated. A 12-volt electrical system was used for the first time, the two separate 6-volt batteries being housed beneath the floor of the rear section. These alterations were sufficient for the car number prefix to be raised from 3T to 4T.

Prices remained fairly constant between 1926 and 1927, during which time the Twelve–Four production was expanded by 55 per cent [*actually 40 per cent, from 10,000 to 14,000, see table in appendix*]. Incidentally, the increase in mechanisation now meant that, on average, only 10 employees were required to produce one car per week in 1927, compared with 55 in 1922. The long-stroke 4T chassis was reduced by £20 to £225 and a new tourer, the Open Road, was brought out at £50 more than the Clifton, now becoming somewhat old in style. The Open Road had separately adjustable front seats in place of the Clifton's double bucket bench seat, and sophisticated side screens which folded down into recesses in the doors. Although first pictured in the March 1927 catalogue, the production records state that the first Open Road was not produced until October of the following year [*the Open Road was included in the catalogue from November 1926, and survivors are known which were registered in December 1926*]. The Windsor and the Iver were still popular, costing £350 and £370, the latter being available in Royal Blue, Monitor Grey, Smoke Blue, Auto Brown, or Maroon. Mulliners still offered the two-four seater and the saloon in blue, grey or maroon. Gordon offered the saloon landaulet with and without division, and Hoyal, the three-seater coupé.

The Austin Twelve, from £275 to £405 were not the cheapest of cars, this demand being catered for by the Seven, but they were certainly well made, excellent value and totally dependable and, as such, successfully upheld their market position until 1929, in spite of some self-imposed competition from the Austin 16/6.

From October 1927 the car began to lose some of its charm, and so grew to provide more room and greater comfort. The 5T series from August 1927 had its track increased by 4in to 4ft 8in (1422mm), and the radiator cowl was raised: These modifications were necessary to allow for the new six-cylinder engine. It was hoped that the 12 and the new 16 would be produced together and that as the 16 was to cost only £40 more than the 12, sales of the 16 would gradually increase at the expense of the smaller-engined model. In fact, although the 16 was an excellent engine, it never really did as well as had been hoped. The 12 just refused to die, rather like the Morris 1000 of more recent times, and the demand remained just sufficient to keep it in production for longer than would normally have been the case.

By October 1928 the means by which the car was re-fuelled was changed to a telescopic tube which extended out from under the driver's seat, making it no longer necessary to remove the driver's seat to refuel or examine the fuel gauge. I have never discovered why it took them no less than six years to make this very simple modification.

The chassis now cost only £185, the Clifton £245, the special two-seater and the Open Road £265, the Burnham £315 [*this was the new saloon which was designed for the six cylinder engine*], and there were the new fabric saloons, brought out in 1927, which were very fashionable for a short time. The body simply consisted of stretched and padded cellulose-covered cloth over a flexible wooden frame, was free from rattle, it was light and easy to clean. It was meant to be durable, but its lasting qualities were less than that of a metal body, and it rotted quite rapidly. The result being a heap of rattling sticks held together by rotting canvas. Austin figures show the typical fabric saloon history. They made 200 in 1927, 1564 in 1928, 874 in 1929, 344 in 1930, and by 1931 the fabric vogue had gone. In 1928 the six-window fabric saloon cost £315 – the same price as the metal Burnham – and the four-window £305. This had an enclosed rear section with imitation pram hood fittings at the side to give the impression of it being a drophead. Mulliners and Gordon continued to offer their own special bodies and, as will be seen from the production figures, there was a surprisingly high demand for better quality bodies.

By 1929 the fuel tank capacity had been increased from 8 to 10 gallons (36 to 45 litres), and in March the old style gate change gear box was replaced by the ball change selector used on the 16/6. Although not as attractive, and no longer strictly "vintage", gear changing on this model was certainly simplified. The complete model range included the Clifton at £250, Open Road and two-four seat special at £270, the four-light fabric at £310, six-light at £320, the Burnham at the same price, and the Iver at £10 more, whilst three Gordon bodies and the Mulliner saloon were still available. The fuel tank was moved to the back of the car in August 1929, and all exterior fittings were chromium-plated from October, whilst at the same time non-lubricated spring shackles and Triplex safety glass became standard.

Having taken to closed cars in place of tourers, the public had second thoughts about fresh air, and all saloons were available with sliding roofs at £5 extra. This addition was more complicated to fit on the Iver because of the division, and the sliding roof on that model cost £10. A new model, the Sportsman's saloon, was listed from June 1929 to March 1930 and was a fabric car with two wide doors, with limited rear seat passenger capacity and a covered boot at the back. It is recorded in the production figures under "other styles", there being no separate section for the Sportsman's saloon, but production in 1929 and early 1930 could not have been more than 25. Prices remained fairly static in 1930 and the following colours were available prior to the introduction of the 6T series in August [*the 6T was actually introduced in about September 1929*]: Open models: Opal Blue, Royal Blue, Brown, Silver Grey; Sportsman and fabric models: Blue, Maroon, Brown and Black; Burnham and Iver: Royal Blue, Electric

Blue with silver line, Maroon, Maroon and Silver Grey, Brown, Brown and Cream [*a typical 1930s combination popular with exterior decorators on private housing estates at that time*], Opal Blue, Silver Grey and Dual Beige.

In October 1930 the Burnham, Iver and Open Road were still being produced, the two-seater became the Eton and the four-light fabric the Marlow saloon; two six-light fabric saloons were catalogued as the Watford and the Wycombe [*the Watford was actually a four-light*]. Upholstery was either leather, furniture hide or moquette. All models had new bulbous front wings, fluted bonnet sides and, much against Herbert Austin's wishes, the closed car windscreens were allowed a very small slope. Austin always maintained that a windscreen ought to be dead upright, and each year his agents and sales staff used to plead for a sloping screen to make the cars more modern in appearance. They fought hard for each degree, but it was a very gradual process.

From 1931 onwards annual production figures for the Twelve never reached 3000. It was simply a 16/6 with a 12hp engine option, the only outward sign being in the pressed steel spoked wheels, wire wheels not being used in conjunction with a Twelve engine until October 1932.

The 1932 catalogue listed only the Burnham at £288 and the new Windsor at £268, this model being the new saloon style for the 16/6. The Sixteen was now only £30 more than the Twelve and it says a lot for either the quality of salesmanship or the buyers' obstinacy that as many as 2600 12s could be sold in that year. Open Road tourers, Harrow two-seaters, Berkeley and Westminster saloons were added to the range in 1932, and by August 1933 even the tourer screens sloped back a little. All models had a new gearbox from September with synchromesh on the intermediate gears, and direction indicators became standard fitments.

In January 1934 the new chassis bore little resemblance to the plain vintage straight-sided frame. It was low slung with a wide sweep up over the rear axle, tapered in at the front and was held rigid by cross-shaped central members. The wheel size was reduced from 20in to 18in and the car was now typical of the mid-30s: the standard chassis wheelbase was 9ft 4in (2845mm), but to accommodate the Iver body style a 10ft (3048mm) wheelbase chassis was used. By August the following models were available with the Twelve engine: Westminster at £325, Berkeley at £295, Iver at £315 and the Carlton at £305. The last catalogue to list the Austin 12 was published in January 1935 and it contained the Westminster, York, Chalfont, and Hertford models.

The last car with the 12.8hp engine was built on 12 December 1936. It bore no resemblance to the car which had been so popular in the 1920s. It had lost its tall upright appearance, its plated radiator shell had been replaced by cowled-in coachwork, but it still retained that steady, reliable engine which was to continue in production until October 1940.

Not that Austin forsook the 12hp market; the old fashioned Twelve was simply replaced by a 1535cc 12, the forerunner of which had appeared in 1933 as the Light 12/4. It joined yet another 12hp choice, as the Light 12/6 which had been introduced early in 1931 in answer to the popular contemporary vogue for small sixes. Although a perfectly satisfactory car, the 12/6 was not a great sales success, being taxed as a 14hp car despite a capacity of only 1496cc. It produced 3bhp less than the Heavy Twelve, it used more fuel, and was very little cheaper at between £200 and £305 in 1933, which incidentally made it between £29 and £90 more expensive than the Light 12/4. Despite its smoothness and flexibility, and its option of a 16hp engine, the 12/6 was discontinued in 1936 in favour of the 12 and 14.

The story of the Heavy Twelve does not end there, it might have done but for the war and the fact that the 12.8 Austin engine was used in the London taxis from 1930 to the end of 1937. With 84,000 Twelves having been built and 5110 Austin taxis made for use in London, all with rugged engines good for 80,000 miles or more without trouble, they were destined to be used for many more years. The last 12/4 taxi was taken out of service around 1954. This was at a time when I became enthusiastic about the Austin Twelve, referred to, somewhat derisively, as the "Heavy" Twelve. Supporters of other marques regarded it as nothing more than a saloon version of the taxi, forgetting that it was only designated "Heavy" in the early years of that decade to distinguish it from the 11.9hp Light 12/4 that ultimately replaced it. The Austin 12 cars were also still in regular use at that time, when a good 12/4 was worth about £50 and a taxi would fetch about £20. Happily, in spite of the low value placed upon them at that time, many hundreds have survived and – having lasted so long – will now continue to give pleasure to future generations.

Author's note: Bob's love of the Austin Twelve-Four acted as the catalyst for the formation of the Vintage Austin Register, when, in 1958 he invited other owners with a similar interest to come together and form a register of all surviving Twelves. Initially called the Vintage Austin Twelve-Four Register, the name was changed a couple of years later when it became apparent that owners of the Austin Sixteen and the Twenty also wished to become members.

Today, with Registers also thriving in New Zealand and Australia, and other Austin clubs around the World, over 1000 Austin Twelves are known to have survived and, as Bob said, they still provide their owners with immense pleasure a century after they were first launched.

Technical description
The chassis

Following on from Bob's opening general history, I shall describe in greater detail many of the areas mentioned within it, commencing with the chassis. On cars manufactured up to 1934 it is described as being of a pressed steel channel section measuring 4.5in by 1.5in (114mm by 38mm) of 6/7 SWG thickness (5/32in or 4mm). It has four pressed and one tubular cross members. The plan view below shows that the two side frames run parallel from the rear to the point where the fronts of the rear springs are attached, and then tapers towards the front.

From January-March 1933 the frames were constructed differently for the new range of vehicles which included the 10/4, Light 12/4, and the 12/6. These are described as cross-braced frames (chassis) and were fitted from chassis number 71751. The illustration shown below was actually for the 10/4, bur other than the overall size was identical to those for the Heavy Twelve-Four cars and the taxicabs.

The engine

The engine fitted to the Twelve-Fours was described as a four-cylinder short-stroke monobloc unit with a detachable head. The cast-iron cylinder block was separate from the aluminium crankcase. It was fitted with aluminium pistons, and from 1921 to 1926 had a bore of 72mm and 102mm stroke. The capacity was 1661cc, and with an RAC rating of 12.8hp the engine generated 20bhp. By October 1926 this engine was replaced by the long-stroke unit which, whilst retaining the 72mm bore had the stroke increased to 114.5mm. The capacity became 1861cc and whilst still a 12.8hp unit, it now generated 27bhp at

Herbert Austin's faithful chauffeur Jack Gethin driving a 1922 production Twelve-Four through the impressive gateway to Toddington Manor, Bedfordshire. (Photo: the late Bob Wyatt)

HISTORY AND TECHNICAL DESCRIPTION

Austin Twelve Chassis, 1927 (with 12 volt electrical system).

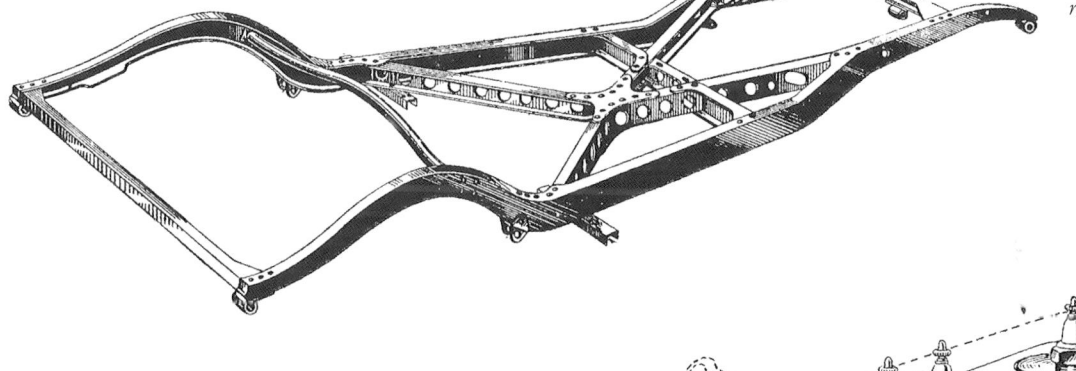

Late cross-braced chassis, rear three-quarter view

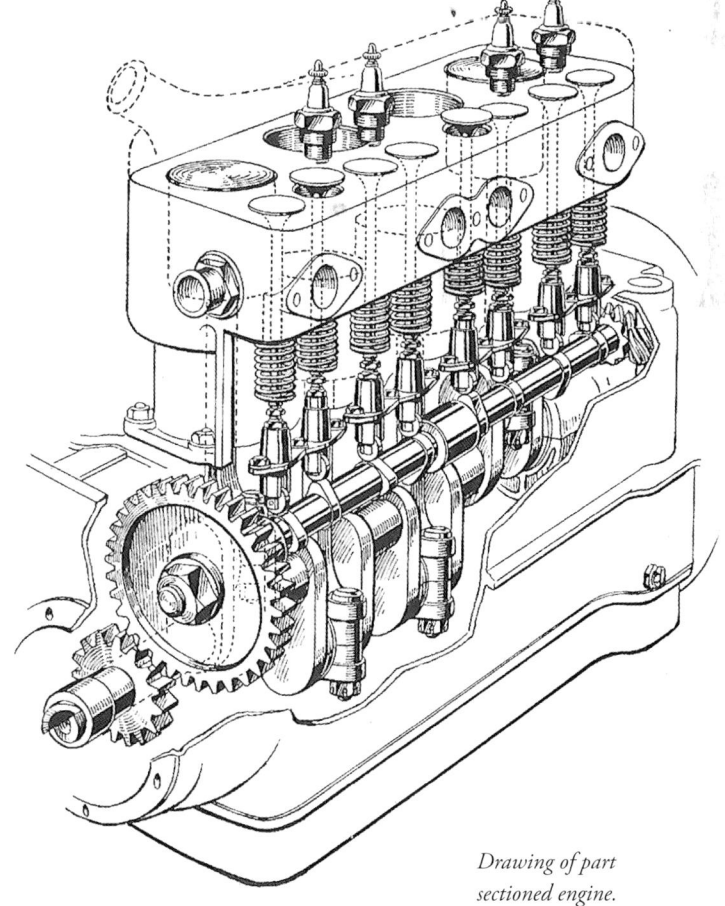

Drawing of part sectioned engine.

2000rpm. From 1934, the catalogue claimed 30bhp at 2600rpm. The long-stroke engine continued to be manufactured up until 1940.

One of the most important features of the Twelve was that the crankshaft had five main bearings, which would not become common on four-cylinder engines until the 1960s. The camshaft was driven by silent chain from a gear at the front of the crankshaft, it was mounted low down on the near-side (left-hand side) and operated side-by-side valves. The same timing chain drove a gearwheel on a shaft for the water pump, in front, and magneto, behind. The carburettor was mounted on the off-side (right-hand side) and the incoming mixture was channelled through two internal passages to the other side of the block.

Fuel system: Autovac and carburettor

Throughout the entire life of the Austin Twelve-Four, the carburettor was fed by an Autovac. As the name implies, the fuel is drawn up from the tank using the vacuum created by the operation of the engine, from where it flows down to the carburettor. The body of the Autovac contains just over a litre of petrol.

The neatly laid out tool tray displaying the complete set of tools originally supplied with all Austin motor cars. (Photo: George McGuire)

The short-stroke engine fitted to a 1926 Clifton tourer. The carburettor is a Zenith 30 HZ type. (Photo: Tony Smallbone)

The choice of carburettor for the first Austin Twelves until late 1924 was the Zenith 30 H, a robust bronze bodied unit with a large float chamber but without a choke. The 30 HZ introduced in 1924 had a smaller float chamber and a choke. When the short-stroke engine was superseded by the long-stroke engine in September 1926, the 30 HZ was slightly modified to suit, with changes to the choke tube and the jets.

On the early type of carburettor the slow running jet was adjusted using a screwdriver, the later ones were provided with a knurled knob which made adjustment a much easier task.

In December 1930, the 30 HZ was replaced with the Zenith U type, or 30 UH which carried on until replaced by the 30 VEH which was in use until the Twelve-Four ceased production. Taxicab engines had a slightly modified version of the 30 VEH, the 50 VEH

A near-side image of the 1928 long-stroke engine showing a coil conversion in place of the magneto. In the top right-hand corner can be seen the vehicle's car and chassis number plates (see appendix). (Photo: George McGuire)

A long-stroke engine from a 1929 Open Road. The drop-down lid to the tool box can clearly be seen adjacent to the Autovac. The carburettor is the Zenith 30 HZ. (Photo: Tony Smallbone)

A near-side image of the 1934 long-stroke engine. (Photo: Dr Damian Tominey)

which was reputed to provide greater economy.

Electrics

The vital spark which ignited the petrol vapour at the spark plugs was supplied by a magneto. Over the life of the Twelve-Four several different types of magnetos from various manufacturers were used, including Watford (type F4, later FM4), Fellows, BLIC, and from 1926, BTH (type Ga4) and the ML types CG4 and RG4 made by the ML Magneto Syndicate Ltd (formerly Morris & Lister), of Coventry. There was also a coil conversion available from the mid-1920s. When introduced, the Sixteen-Six came with coil ignition, but the Twelve-Four continued with magneto ignition until 1934. Coil ignition was introduced with the cowled radiator on 1935 model year cars, and on the taxis about the same time.

The early models had a 6-volt system supplied by C.A.V. and in 1924-25 Remy. In late 1925, the lighting set, switch panel, dashboard lighting, and ammeter were changed to Lucas. By October of 1926 the system was changed to 12 volts, a little later on some export models. Starter motors and dynamos were similarly provided by C.A.V., Remy, or Lucas.

Exterior lighting on the pre 1926 Twelves was supplied by C.A.V and consisted of two nickel-plated stirrup-mounted head lamps which could not be dipped, two nickel-plated side lamps, and one rear light which was mounted so as to illuminate the rear number plate. From late 1925 the lamp configuration remained the same but Austin used Lucas lamps which were enamelled in black, with 7.5in headlamps type R40. In 1928 slightly larger headlamps type R57 were introduced and the front near-side lamp was soon designed to dip by means of a vacuum pump. The off-side lamp was permanently dipped. From May 1930 the dipping mechanism was operated electrically via a solenoid located behind the reflector. The 1931 and later models had "dip and switch" headlamps, sometimes called "Biflex" type.

Trafficators (i.e., direction indicators) began to be fitted to cars from September 1933 for the 1934 model year, but were available earlier as an accessory from Lucas, Desmo, Hunt and several other manufacturers which could be added to earlier cars if required. Stop lamps were introduced in January 1932 and were combined with the rear lamps. Smaller side lamps were fitted from December 1931, and from September 1933 were given a tapered shape and were re-located from a bracket mounted on the scuttle to the top of the front wings. The De-luxe Berkeley saloons had chrome plated lamps whilst the standard Berkeley saloons had lamps which were painted black.

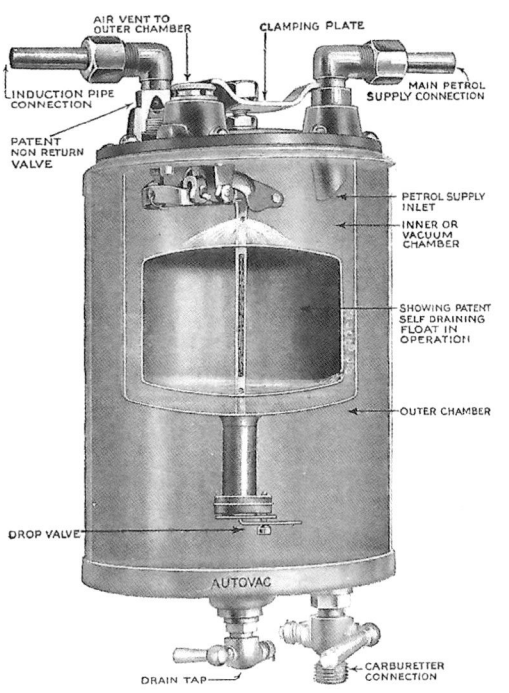

Part-sectioned Autovac from handbook.

Wheels and tyres

The 1921 prototype was fitted with four-stud Michelin disc wheels with 760x90mm beaded edge tyres, but these were discarded on production vehicles in favour of six-stud, twelve spoke artillery wheels fitted with 765x105mm beaded edge tyres. Whilst the rims were made from steel, the spokes were made from hickory wood. They were available well into 1924. In 1923 they began to be replaced with either Sankey or Dunlop ten-spoke steel artillery wheels. On cars with four-wheel brakes from October 1924, 5.00x20in balloon tyres were fitted.

Whilst the Twelve-Four was supplied with the artillery wheels as standard, from 1928 purchasers could request having them replaced with the wire wheels which were fitted as standard to the new Sixteen-Six, for an extra £10. The early wire wheels had small hubs and visible wheel nuts. From September-October 1931 the new type Magna wire wheel with a large hub and wheel nuts concealed by a chrome-plated hub cap began to be introduced on De Luxe models, but at least the new Windsor still had artillery wheels. Magna wheels became standard for the 1934 model year, except on taxicabs which retained the artillery wheels until production ceased in 1940.

Transmission

Drive from the engine is taken through a clutch and gearbox mounted in unit with the engine, then through an open prop shaft (the so-called "Hotchkiss" drive) to the rear axle.

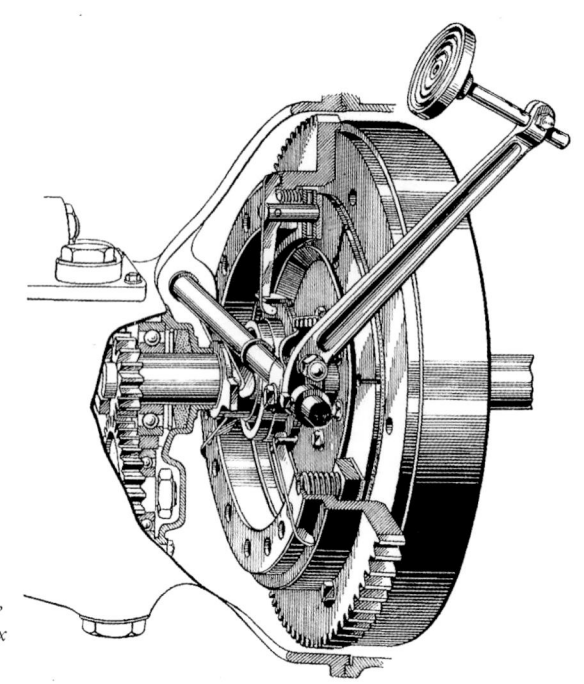

Line drawings of clutch, and of sectioned gearbox from handbook.

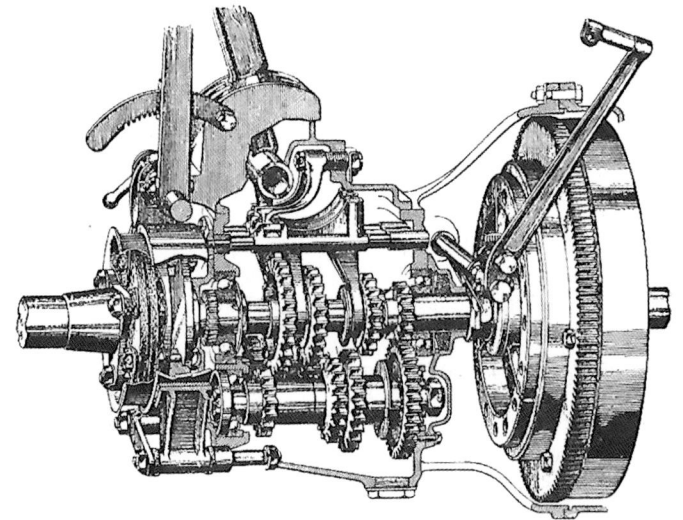

The clutch is the dry single plate type and is connected directly between the end of the engine crankshaft and the gearbox. Depressing the clutch pedal releases the friction disc away from the steel plate which disconnects the engine from the gearbox.

The Austin Twelve-Four gearbox is of the sliding mesh type and is fitted with four forward and one reverse gear. The gears are mounted on shafts which may be described as first, second and third motion shafts. The first motion shaft (or engine shaft) is attached directly to the clutch and carries just one gear. It drives the front gearwheel on the second motion shaft (or layshaft). Three further gearwheels on the layshaft mesh in turn with three different sliding gears on the third motion shaft (or mainshaft) to give different gear ratios for first, second, and third gears. The mainshaft drives the prop shaft. In top gear the engine shaft is locked to the mainshaft, giving direct drive. Reverse is obtained by sliding a separate idler gear between the first gear pair of gears on the layshaft and mainshaft.

The early Twelve-Four gearboxes did not have synchromesh, so when changing gear, the clutch had to be depressed twice, known as double declutching, with a short pause in neutral, in order to allow the speed of the engine to match that of the gears, otherwise the gear change will be very noisy.

The early Twelves had a short gear lever with a visible gate for the gear positions. This can be clearly seen in the illustration under brakes. The small lever just below the gear lever knob must be operated to engage reverse gear. This was referred to as the gate change box. By March 1929 this gearbox was superseded by the ball change box which had a longer gear stick, but still no synchromesh. A synchromesh gearbox was introduced on cars and taxicabs manufactured from chassis number 74372 in September 1933. It had third and top gears in constant mesh and was described as the "Twin-Top" gearbox, as the change between top and third gears was made easy by the synchromesh. A year later second gear was also given synchromesh.

The rear axle

The rear axle is attached to the gearbox by the propeller or prop shaft, connected to the gearbox by a fabric coupling, and to the axle via a metal universal joint known as the pot joint. This allows for any end play and sideways movement.

The rear axles fitted to Austin Twelve-Fours are known as the three-quarter floating type, in which the wheel hub is partly supported by ball bearings and partly by its connection with the axle. The inner ends of each half shaft are supported in plain roller bearings. Final drive is by spiral bevel.

Lubrication is maintained through a filler hole at the rear of the axle, set at the maximum level of oil in the axle; overfilling results in the oil flowing back out. It is worth noting that the date when the completed chassis left the chassis assembly shop to have the bodywork fitted is stamped on the axle in this area. Both front and rear axles were changed for cars manufactured from September 1933.

Brakes

Initially the Austin Twelve-Four was equipped with foot brakes which only operated on the rear wheels,

HISTORY AND TECHNICAL DESCRIPTION

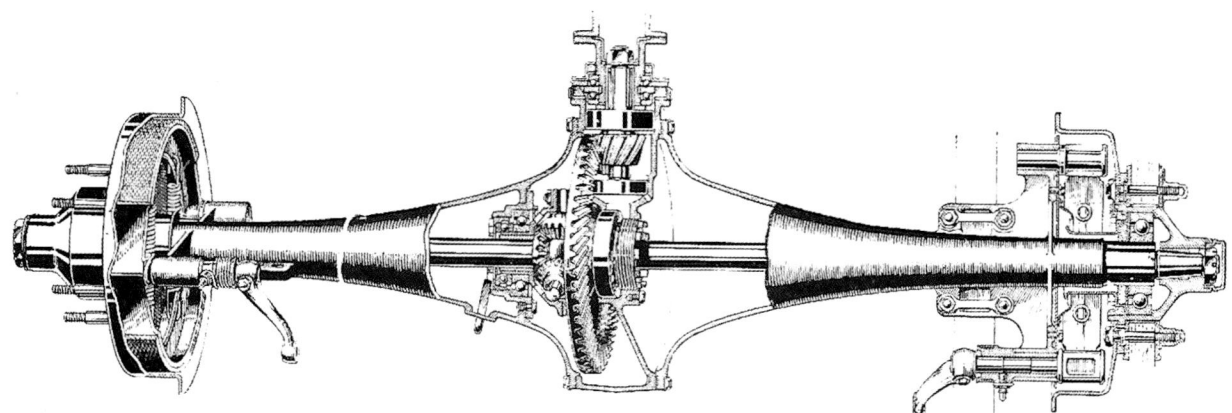

Above: Line drawing of part-sectioned rear axle from handbook.

and a very effective transmission hand brake. Front wheel brakes were introduced from October 1924.

The first of the two illustrations show the gearbox from the rear where the gear change lever is located in its gate. The hand brake lever operates two shoes, which, when the lever is pulled backwards, press against a drum mounted on the extension of the gearbox mainshaft immediately behind the gearbox. The application of this brake prevents the prop shaft and rear wheels from turning. The second illustration shows the front brake mechanism. The brakes are activated through a series of rods and cables when the brake pedal is depressed.

Steering and suspension

The steering of the Austin Twelve-Four was through what is known as a worm and wheel gearbox. The worm is located in the steering box at the base of the steering column. This engages with the wheel which moves the steering arm backwards or forwards causing the track rod to alter the direction of the road wheels. The actual steering box was bolted on the inside of the chassis side member. On early cars with the 4ft track, the shaft from the box to the drop arm protruded through the chassis so the drop arm was on the outside, as can be seen in the chassis illustration from the 1922 brochure in chapter 7. These cars had the unsightly drop-arm cover inserted in the front wing. On cars with the wider track, the drop arm was moved to the inside of the steering box.

All four road springs were semi-elliptic. From 1928 the leaves were separated by thin zinc interleaves. The springs were mounted on shackles with phosphor bronze bushes, the shackles on later models were fitted with Silentbloc bushes which, unlike earlier ones, did not require lubrication. Early models were fitted with Hartford friction dampers which were replaced by Smith's shock absorbers in 1929 (or on some cars, Armstrongs on the rear). Later still, the Hartfords were re-introduced.

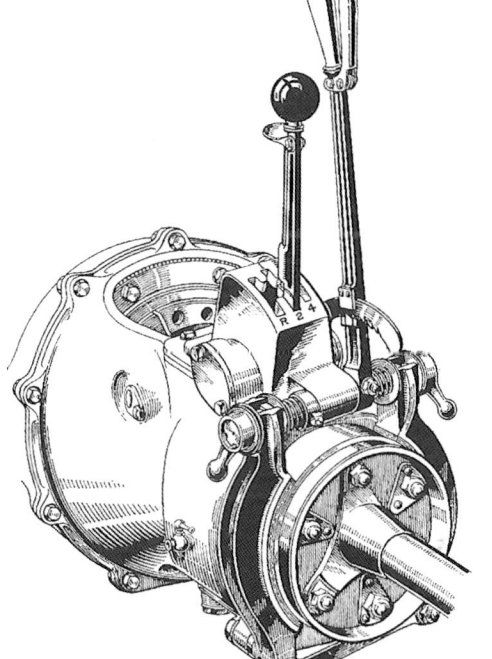

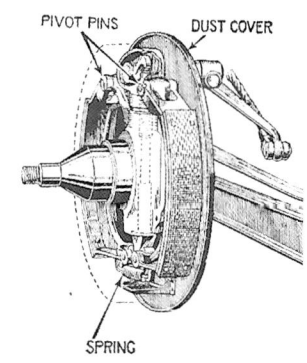

Above and left : Line drawings of gearbox showing handbrake, and front brake drum, from handbook.

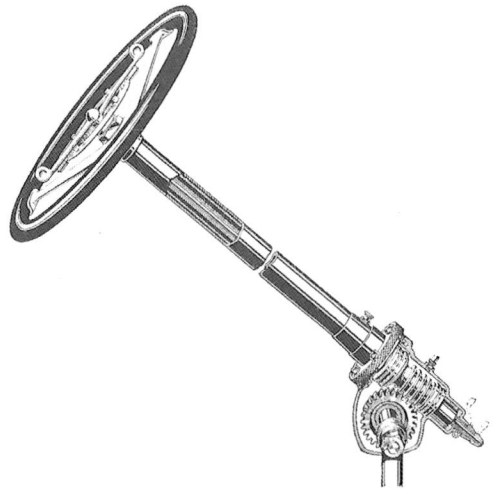

Line drawing of steering wheel, column, and gearbox, from handbook.

17

Dash and Instruments

The instrument panel from 1922 tourer. Note metal dash and no glove pockets. (Photo: Peter Wright)

The instrument panel from a 1924 Windsor saloon, now with glove pockets at both ends, and white-faced instruments. (Photo: Peter Wright)

A typical dashboard layout for the 6-volt Twelve-Four of 1926 (June/September). (Photo: Tony Smallbone)

On a 1934 Twelve-Four Iver saloon the clock and the speedometer (far right) are now at each end of the dash, with the smaller instruments and switchgear on a metal panel. (Photo: Dr Damian Tominey

Instrument panel from a 12-volt Open Road tourer of 1929 with black-faced instruments. (Photo: Tony Smallbone)

HISTORY AND TECHNICAL DESCRIPTION

Interior

The interior trim on all Austin motor cars was always of the highest quality. The seats were finished in best quality Connolly Vaumol leather, or hard wearing furniture hide for open cars. There was also a choice of Moquette or Bedford Cord for rear passenger compartments. The seats on earlier cars were generally "buttoned", then from 1928 fluted. The headlining was always made from West of England cloth, and the carpets best quality Wilton. The illustrations below show just a few interior shots, some of which are original and others which may have been re-trimmed to the original specification.

Clifton tourer buttoned upholstery. (Photo: Peter Moyle)

Semi-buttoned & fluted upholstery on Windsor Saloon. (Photo: Tony Smallbone)

Fluted leather upholstery on a 1929 fabric saloon. (Photo by author)

From the 1922 Austin Twelve Spare Parts List, the list and illustrations of the complete set of tools which were supplied with each car.

The near-side front door panel on a 1929 fabric saloon. (Photo by author)

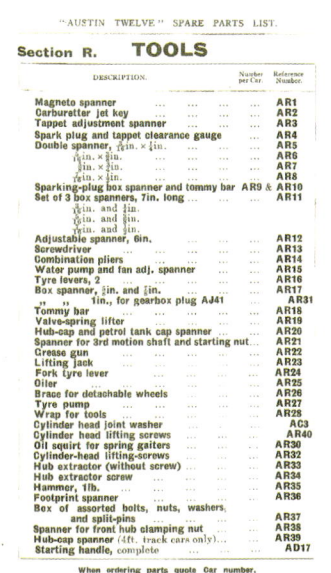
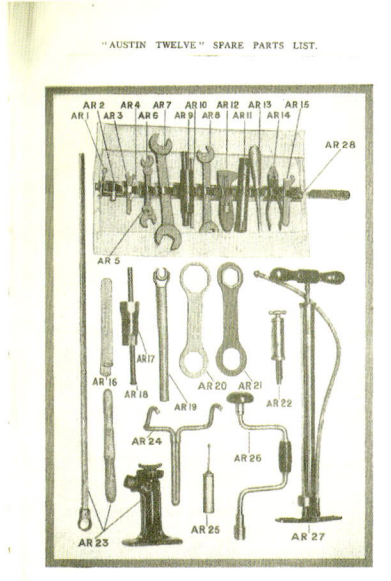

Chapter Two

THE MOTORING PRESS AND THE AUSTIN TWELVE

Three-quarter front shot of the 1921 prototype tourer on disc wheels.

The earliest road test of the Austin Twelve-Four was carried out by *The Autocar* magazine and reported on in their edition for 1 October 1921, a few months before the car was officially launched. Further road tests were reported on in the pages of *The Motor* and later, in the *Austin Advocate*. But first, this is what the reporter from *The Autocar* had to say:

The Autocar has a scoop
"The Austin Twelve: Lines of the larger car followed in a general Utility Design, provided with a four-speed Gear Box and a Thorough Equipment.

Considerable importance may be attached to the introduction of the Austin Twelve. Not only is it the offspring of what we may term "Blood Stock", but its birthplace at Northfield is at once one of the most important and one of the largest motor manufacturing plants in the Kingdom. From these two facts, to which may be added the excellent reputation that some thousand post-war Austin Twenties have gained for themselves. It will be seen that this new and smaller model is one deserving more than ordinary consideration. Broadly speaking the aims of the Austin Co. have been to produce a car of popular dimensions at a popular price that will cater strictly for the needs of the user who desires to motor in comfort at moderate cost.

"It is the outcome of an increasing demand which manufacturers have felt for the past twelve months to be undeniable; the demand for sheer value as against mere beauty of outline and ostentatious performance, for the family car which may be relied upon to render efficient and absolutely reliable service with the very minimum of unskilled attention from the owner, who is generally the driver.

"At first glance one cannot help remarking – before any other impression asserts itself – the similarity of this latest model and the larger car which bears the same name. Externally everything about it, the bonnet, wings, screen and general body lines – is the same, and, although we believe the desire of the manufacturers is that the Austin Twelve should be regarded as an entirely special production, it is obvious that those points of construction which have proved themselves sound in the Austin Twenty have been incorporated in miniature in the smaller model. As the illustrations show, the engine is commendably neat, every part being immediately accessible for adjustment without the previous necessity of removing some other component. With a bore and stroke of 72x102mm (1661cc), the power output of approximately 20bhp, is obtained at 2000rpm.

"The head is detachable, and in practically every

respect follows that trend of design which of late has been adopted by a number of leading manufacturers. Both inlet and exhaust valves are on the left hand side of the cylinder block, and are enclosed behind aluminium covers on the same side. Driven by silent chain from the crankshaft is the magneto, mounted on an adjustable bracket, which may be swung outwards in order to tighten the chain by loosening a locking ring behind a knurled thumb screw on the timing wheel cover. In a similar manner the spindle of the fan is carried on an eccentric so as to provide adjustment for its flat belt, the latter being driven from a pulley on the end of the dynamo driving spindle, an important point being that the dynamo is rotated by an enclosed chain.

"Cooling is effected by a standard pattern water pump situated opposite the magneto on the forward side of the timing case, and it will be observed that large diameter water pipes have been adopted. The entire engine and gear box unit are mounted in a frame on the three-point attachment system, which allows for some slight lateral movement when the car is turning corners or running on a steep camber of the road. The well-tried principles of lubrication which have proved successful on the 20hp model have been adopted. Oil is fed by means of a gear pump to the main bearings and through the usual channels in the crankshaft webs to the big ends, the cylinders being served by splash. Special provision has been made for filtering the oil on its way to the various bearings, etc., and the filter is easily removable. The oil level is very simply indicated by means of a dipper rod fitted with a maximum and minimum level collars; whilst the oil pressure is shown by a gauge on the dashboard.

Gearbox and Transmission

"To the rear of the engine the gear box is bolted through the intermediary of the bell housing open at the top but surrounding the single plate clutch and flywheel. A point about the gear box upon which we would lay stress is that four forward speeds are given. This is a wise provision, for there can be no doubt that, no matter how good a small car with a three speed box may be, in the hands of an intelligent driver it is better with four speeds. On the Austin Twelve a central lever with a gate change is used, together with a central brake lever which takes effect upon contracting shoes applied to a drum on the gear box driven shaft and made easily adjustable to take up wear. Both brake and clutch pedals are carried as part of the unit, and below their assembly the electric starting motor is spigoted into the flywheel housing. It is interesting to observe that a positive gear drive for the speedometer is encased at the back of the gearbox.

"Within the transmission brake drum is contained a handy flexible disc joint, from which an open propeller shaft can proceed to the rear axle, the latter having a spiral bevel final drive and shafts of the semi-floating type, *i.e.,* part of the weight of the car is taken on the axle casing and part on the shafts. Expanding shoe brakes are placed in drums on the rear wheel hubs, and the set is operated by a pedal. The suspension of the chassis is carried out on long semi-elliptic springs of 4ft, and 2ft 8in respectively, the rear springs being under slung and the front springs mounted above the axle.

"As regards the fuel supply, an eight-gallon tank is situated beneath the driver's seat and held by brackets on the frame alongside the driving shaft. The carburettor is fed from the tank by an Autovac mounted on the dashboard. The batteries are stowed away in a box carried in a similar manner to the fuel tank on the opposite side of the propeller shaft.

Concerning the Coachwork

"Turning from the chassis proper, the bodywork claims attention on the score of its workmanlike appearance and the real comfort which it affords. There is ample leg room even for a tall passenger in both front seats, and the upholstery, which is carried out in green leather, is comfortable. The front seat is made adjustable; the one-man hood folds compactly and has a dust cover, the windscreen is of the adjustable two-panel variety, and the wings are domed. One spare Michelin wheel is supplied, and is carried at the rear of the car between the dumb irons on a very neat cast bracket fitted with four studs, to which the wheel is bolted, in precisely the same way as when on the road. This bracket is so arranged that two spare wheels can be carried if desired.

"Another interesting point is the manner in which both brackets for side and head lamps may be adjusted upwards, downwards and sideways to secure the best results for night driving in different parts of the country.

"From the above description it will be seen that little has been left out of the specification of the Austin Twelve which could render it more serviceable to the owner or more comfortable to the passenger, but at the same time nothing has been added to its equipment which could in any way be called superfluous . The car is precisely what the designers intend it to be – a utility vehicle of attractive appearance and efficient performance.

The Car on the Road

"We gave the car a brief test over some average roads in the Bromsgrove district – roads that were neither good nor bad, but which allowed one to form a preliminary estimate of the car's qualities. Chiefly we were impressed by the silence of the engine at low speeds. As regards general riding comfort, it would be difficult to find any reasonable complaint. The cushions might possibly be wider, but we believe that this point is to be rectified in production models. The springing at all speeds was good, and the steering as it should be. The transmission is silent; the rear axle emits no more than a pleasant hum which one associates with a newly assembled unit. The car proved capable of a fair turn of speed, whilst the engine was flexible, and smooth running within the range commonly used in ordinary driving.

"To sum up, our candid opinion of the new Austin 12hp. is a favourable one, particularly in view of the price, which, we understand, is to be approximately £550. It will be understood, of course, that this new type in no way supersedes the popular Austin Twenty."

The Motor's first test report

And then in their 1 February edition of 1922. *The Motor* magazine reported on the Austin Twelve as follows:

"The new Austin Twelve in many respects stands out from the vehicles of a similar type. In the first place, the four seated touring body affords greater accommodation than is usually found on a chassis of only 9ft 4in wheelbase. Another excellent feature is that the backs of both front and rear seats come well up to the shoulders, a detail which appreciably affects the comfort of the occupants on a journey of any length.

"Thanks to the sliding front seats and the adjustable pedals it is possible to suit the new light Austin to a driver of any build. The upholstery, which is of real leather is deep and restful, and is supported in the case of the seat cushions, on springs that afford a high degree of insulation without being unduly "bouncy" or lively.

Well-constructed Coachwork

"Owing to the central position of the gear and brake levers, unrestricted access is provided on the off-side. The high-sided body seems entirely rigid and the doors are mounted in such a way as should effectually obviate any tendency to rattle. The spare wheel is carried at the rear of the body, where it is out of the way of luggage.

"Turning to the mechanical aspects of the Austin Twelve, the four-cylinder monobloc engine, which measures 72mm by 102mm (1660 cc) is interesting in that its crankshaft is supported by no fewer than five main bearings, which, in conjunction with the unit construction of gearbox and locomotive-type external contracting transmission brake, makes for complete and permanent axial rigidity and freedom from whip. The application of what may be termed the auxiliary mechanism, i.e., dynamo, starter, magneto etc., is neatly carried out, while the general finish is unusually good.

"The single plate clutch is light to operate and progressive in action. Indeed it is possible to start away from rest in top gear without racing the engine and without slipping the clutch for more than a dozen yards. The ability of the engine to hang onto the top gear of 5.2 to 1 is little short of extraordinary, and may certainly be said to be well above the average for an engine of similar capacity. The other gears are 7.5, 12.2 and 19.3 to 1. The brakes are good. We were very favourably impressed with the steering, which was delightfully light, and at the same time seemed fully irreversible.

"The acceleration of the new Austin Twelve provided us with an entirely new experience. The way the car, with a load of four passengers, shot forward from a sedate 20mph on pressing the accelerator pedal, seemed entirely out of keeping with the type of car. It can best be likened to the performance of an ultra-efficient sports model with a light two-seater body.

"The range of speed on top gear on the particular car tried by us may be put down as from 4mph to just over 40mph, although we understand that that a speed of over 50mph has been attained on the same model fitted with a modified form of carburettor.

"Perhaps the outstanding feature of the light Austin is the suspension, which is so good as to suggest the riding of a first-grade car many sizes larger. Particularly noteworthy is the operation of the back springs, which properly insulate the occupants of the rear seats from road shock on a surface indented with a succession of bad potholes.

Good All-weather Equipment

"The one-man hood which, when out of use, lies quite flat, can be erected single-handed with a minimum of effort. With the side curtains in place, the occupants of the "Austin Twelve" are thoroughly protected from the elements. The side curtains, as is now almost universal, open with the doors. The fact that the lower panel of the screen is also capable of adjustment adds very materially to the driver's comfort, as a combination of the two planes can be found to meet almost any form of weather conditions.

"The engine, which is fitted with aluminium pistons, is entirely devoid of rattle and mechanical noises Economy in running should be a very strong point of this new model, as, in our hands, with a full load and the hood up, the average petrol consumption worked out at slightly in excess of 20 mpg. The appearance of the car leaves nothing to be desired, the outline being

Side view of early production tourer. (Photo from the Austin Advocate*)*

neat and symmetrical.

"The somewhat heavy aspect given to the car by the disc wheels will be done away with in future models, which, we understand, will be fitted with artillery wheels. Tool accommodation has been well studied, with special pockets, situated on either side under the scuttle dash, carrying the detachable starting handle and the wheel brace, while the jack is accommodated at the back of the front seats in a special compartment, the lid of which forms a convenient footrest for the rear passengers.

"Taking it all round, the new "Austin Twelve" represents good value for money at the price of £550, which includes full electrical lighting and starting equipment, clock, and speedometer. And five 765mm by 105mm wheels and tyres.

"The address of the Austin Motor Co., Ltd, is Northfield, Birmingham, while their London depot, through whose courtesy the car was placed at our disposal, is at 479, Oxford Street, London, W.1."

The *Austin Advocate*:
The Company's own publication

In the February-March 1922 edition of the *Austin Advocate* magazine, photographs of the Twelve's body styles were shown followed by what one might describe as a review, then, following on in the June-July edition, an in-depth road test was duly reported where it is interesting to note that within just a few months of *The Autocar* and *The Motor* reports several changes had been made by the Company, specifically with regard to the wheels which were now more in line with the later examples. The reporter, identified simply as LAB, commences his report thus:

Testing the Twelve –
(Assurance doubly assured)

"I shall never be content now until I own an Austin car of my own. Recently I watched and took part in the tests for an Austin Twelve, and I am satisfied – more than satisfied. For a long while I have written praise of the Twelve because I believed it, but now I know. I had ridden in one on several occasions previously, but only quietly touring, doing, in fact, what any other car could do. On test, however, we performed feats that I verily believe no other car dared ever to attempt. But I am beginning my story with the last chapter. The first test takes place in the engine test house. Here the assembled engine is connected with a hydraulic dynamometer that registers the brake horsepower developed at various engine speeds. The tester allows the engine to run for about half-an-hour and then makes any adjustments that are necessary. These are remarkably few and far between. All that had to be done to the engine I observed under test was to fit a new set of piston rings and slightly adjust the tappet clearance. I afterwards saw the same engine mounted in a chassis and was told that it would now have to undergo a continuous running test. As I was already convinced of the capabilities of the engine I did not wait for this.

Shaking Her Up

"Next morning I returned to the testing shop in time to

Test driver making adjustments to the engine of a chassis running on trade plates. (Photo from the Austin Advocate*)*

The test driver on a bare chassis climbing a test hill. (Photo from the Austin Advocate*)*

find the chassis equipped in readiness for its road test, and mounted on the flimsy seat beside the driver with many qualms as to my safety in the immediate future. He depressed the clutch pedal, slipped her into reverse, and we backed gently out through the narrow gateway. I was folding my arms complacently, pleased to find that testing a car was so comfortable after all, when a sudden sickening lurch forward caused me to grab the seat with one hand and my hat with the other, or I should assuredly have parted with both. Another lurch, that nearly threw me right off, and we were careering wildly along the road at 50mph, with the wind roaring in our ears and every nerve and instinct keyed up to respond to the magic touch of speed. The absence of windscreen of course considerably enhanced this effect. After a few miles of this the driver slowed down and turned into a narrow lane with a terrible road surface. "This will find out any loose bolts", he remarked as he again opened out, and the needle trembled at over 35. There it stayed too, while we bumped along, this poor scribe trying hard to register sensations, but finding his whole time occupied in clinging on to the treacherous-looking soap-box-like seat.

Over the Top

"A lengthy stop, while the driver went carefully all around the chassis looking for faults – without success, I may mention – and we headed for the test hill and home. This part of the test really seemed superfluous to me. The hill is a very stiff one indeed but we flew over the crest in top gear without a falter, and the engine running as smoothly and quietly as if we were touring gently along on the level.

"There was no sensation of climbing at all: it was as if the road was horizontal, but some absurd person had built all the houses at a sharp angle, and so home. Concerning this day's test, one thing stands out indisputable. I had gone out with the feeling that testing a stripped chassis on the road was a thing of tradition, surrounded with a soft haze of the glamour of romance. Romance there certainly is, but the test consists, first and foremost, of material realities. The driver's idea is to put a tremendous strain on every part of the chassis, so that not the tiniest defect can escape unnoticed. And very thoroughly and conscientiously does he carry this out.

"Two days later the body was completed, and I was invited to observe the final, the "finished car" test. And in truth it was a test. Such a drive I have never pictured in the most tangential exuberances of imagination. We seemed to get right away from civilisation in a wild, wonderful country of ghastly roads and impossible hills, where road construction was a necessity but road destruction a habit.

A Nightmare Ride

"We sped along the lane 4ft 6in wide at an average speed of 40mph. The road was marked over its entire surface of loose stones with pot holes, some of which were a yard across and 18in deep, while to complete the picture there was the most perfect pair of cart ruts I have ever seen, quite a foot deep. We were walled in on either side by steep clay banks, so that the slightest deviation from the track would have meant that this account would probably never have been written. And then the hills! One that we climbed had the amazing gradient of 1 in 3 for its last 30 yards. To climb it was like leaping at the edge of the world. Nor must I forget a word of praise for the driver. His skill seemed to be nothing short of supernatural. He knew to a quarter of an inch where he wanted the car to be, and he got it there every time. In one place the lane was too narrow for the car, so we went through with two wheels up the bank, he nonchalantly driving with one hand.

The Right Conclusion

"In time we returned to the Works. I had seen all the tests for the "Austin Twelve" and henceforth I am an ardent admirer of its qualities. That the car of medium power and price should combine comfort, speed and hill climbing capabilities in such generous measure is a real tribute to Austin methods and ideas. I can only hope that some day I, who am poor and therefore sound my aitches, shall join the ranks of satisfied "Austin Twelve" owners."

The three reports are interesting in that both the testers from *The Autocar* and *The Motor* Magazines went about their job in a constructive and professional manner, whilst LAB, who wrote the report for the *Austin Advocate* appeared to record his findings in a more relaxed manner. I am not sure about the authenticity of the final drive down the narrow lane with the deep cart tracks and pot holes. Maybe the driver did show off in the manner suggested, but I somehow doubt that he did.

A car for medical men?

Strangely enough, hot on the heels of *The Autocar*'s review, a review albeit brief, appeared in the *British Medical Journal* of 12 November 1921 with the following report:

"The 12-hp Austin car, the introduction of which was announced in these columns a short while ago, is not displayed at the current exhibition, but at the firm's large headquarters in Oxford Street. The design follows closely that of the now well-proved 20-hp. Model. The new product is notable for the amplitude of the body accommodation and for its pleasing lines. In fact, it is a typical Austin-product brought now well within the purse range of the average medical man. The engine is not highly stressed, and the wearing qualities should, in consequence, be excellent. It is unusual, too, among machines of this rating from the fact that the gear-box gives four speeds forward."

The Motor follows up

The next report was published some fourteen months later in *The Motor* dated 27 February 1923. In their report entitled "The 1923 Austin Twelve, Road Test of a Well-equipped Medium-sized Family Car" they had this to say:

"All who are thinking of purchasing a medium-sizes touring car should give careful consideration to the Austin Twelve. It is exceptionally roomy for an engine rated at 12.8hp. It bristles with points that appeal to the owner-driver; the suspension is far above the average of cars of its class and it has the performance of a more powerful vehicle, without the expense. Considering the excellence of the chassis, completeness of the bodywork and equipment, it represents extraordinarily good value, and it is not surprising to learn that it is even more popular than the famous Austin Twenty.

"We have recently carried out a road test of the 1923 model. The variations from the original specification are very slight, the most notable being that the wheel track has been increased to 4ft 4in, thus making it more suitable for overseas use while affording greater stability on the road. When supplied from the London depot of the Austin Motor Company Ltd., 479-483, Oxford Street, W.1, it was absolutely new, and, therefore not quite equal to the performance expected from it after another 500 miles.

"The Austin Twelve is equipped with C.A.V. starting and lighting, which includes the well-known Willard battery. We found that even from dead cold it could be readily started at the first or second depression of the starter switch without priming or the use of the starting handle. There was no need to wait for the engine to warm up before engaging the gears, although the speed and acceleration improved after the first few miles, especially when the temperature – as was the case when the car was under test – was in the neighbourhood of 40 degrees [*Note: Fahrenheit; about 4.5 degrees Centigrade*].

Gears and hill climbing.

"There is a four-speed gearbox with central control. Gear changing is particularly easy; dead-silent changes, without having to wait a lengthy period when changing up, could be effected without trouble. A single-plate clutch takes up the drive perfectly sweetly and needs no delicate touch on the pedal. We invariably used second speed for starting off, even on hills, the first speed being intended purely as a reserve gear for the emergency negotiation of exceptional hills. The worst gradient encountered was Pebble Coombe, which was coated with tacky mud. This was taken from a standing start at the bend, on second speed, except for the last few yards, when it was deemed advisable to change down to first, finishing the climb at 10mph on this gear.

"We should say that with the engine a little more run in, the hill could easily have been negotiated on second all of the way, and probably the first speed would only be required on gradients steeper than 1 in 5. Easy inclines, say, of 1 in 15 can be taken at very good speed indeed: Kingston Hill, for instance was covered at 38mph, and that sharp, steep rise known as Telegraph Hill, between Hook and Leatherhead, at 35mph. Owing to traffic the car had to be brought to a standstill half way up Kingston Hill, and the speed mentioned was obtained by rapidly changing from second to third and top.

"On the road the most notable feature of the Austin Twelve is that it has the 'feel' and silent running of a higher priced and more powerful car. The engine is quiet and, apparently, has no period; there is no howl from the gears. Indeed, so silent is the running that one has to be on the alert and constantly to sound the horn when passing pedestrians, cyclists, and vehicular traffic.

"There was no opportunity for testing the maximum speed. We had to be content with 42mph, with something in reserve. We understand that the maximum speed is between 45-50mph.

Front and rear seats equally comfortable

"Among the most delightful features of the car are the comfort of the bodywork and the excellence of the suspension, while the passengers are equally insulated from road shocks in the front or the rear seats. Over a bad pot holey road there is only a gentle swaying motion, no violent shocks at all. It holds the road well on corners, and the steering is light. We found that the petrol consumption worked out as near as possible to 30mpg: the oil consumption was not measurable and, like most modern cars, the sump supply should be changed after a certain lapse of time, instead of replenished.

"The controls fall very readily to the hand, and we particularly liked the position of the brake lever. The foot brake, which operates in large drums on the rear wheels, is more progressive and smoother in its action. The combination seems to be an excellent one.

Turning now to its special features

"We have in the first place a very roomy substantially constructed four-five-seater body, with adjustable front seats. The range of adjustment is no less than 6 inches. With the seats right back, which would only be necessary in the case of a very long-legged driver, there is a space between the backs of the front seats and the front edge of the rear seat squab of 20 inches., which, as comparative measurements will show, gives quite comfortable leg room. There is a foot rest for the rear passengers. The width of the rear seat is 43½ inches between the upholstered sides. The front seats are slightly narrower, but there is ample room for two. The body has four doors.

Stiffening the body sides

"A point worthy of note is that unlike most four-seaters with adjustable front seats, the side panels are not left unsupported. They are actually braced, or stiffened, by the backs of the seats from which an iron stay on each side engages with a metal groove on the body panels. To move the seats, two nuts, one on each side-have to be loosened, and the central lever between the squabs released. The front seat squabs are separately detachable – one covering the petrol tank which holds eight gallons and is provided with a gauge, and the other, the batteries. The backs of the seats, either front or rear, are just about the right height and section, affording a natural and restful position.

"The Special model is fitted with a rear screen. The front screen is of the two-panel type, the panels being adjustable. The rear screen is an Auster.

"The hood is easily erected by one person, and is instantly secured by spring catches on the front windscreen frame. Celluloid side panels are provided and carried in a pocket behind the front seats; they convert the car to practically an enclosed one.

"The spare wheel is carried at the rear, together with a very substantial folding luggage carrier. There is space to carry two spare wheels if desired, and so that they shall be easily accessible the luggage carrier is made to pull out.

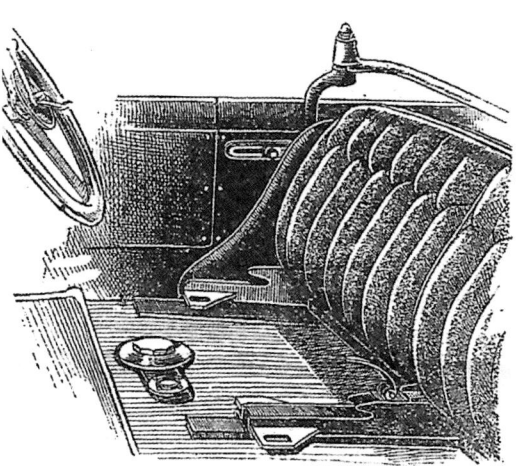

Petrol tank filler located directly under the driver's seat. (Illustration from The Book of the Austin Twelve *by Garbutt & Twelvetrees)*

Rear end with spare wheel and luggage rack. (Illustration from The Book of the Austin Twelve *by Garbutt & Twelvetrees)*

Location of clock on dashboard and tool box under dash of early Twelve-Four. (Illustration from The Book of the Austin Twelve *by Garbutt & Twelvetrees)*

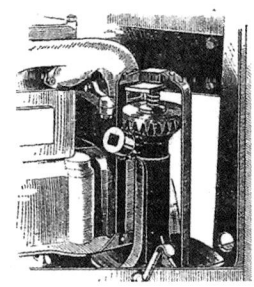

Location of jack. (Illustration from The Book of the Austin Twelve *by Garbutt & Twelvetrees)*

"All the appointments of the car are excellent in appearance and quality. There is a range of standard colours, with leather upholstery, either antique or plain finish, to tone. A particularly striking combination is Kingfisher Blue, with plated fittings, and black wings and valences.

"The equipment includes, apart from the details mentioned, C.A.V. lighting and starting, the head lamps being adjustable; a very handsomely appointed facia board, including Smith speedometer and clock, lighting switchboard, magneto cut out, oil gauge and dash light; Rappa spring gaiters; Zenith carburettor, Enots grease gun lubricating system; Dunlop cord tyres, 765mm by 105mm (these large tyres for a car of this size are a commendable feature), Autovac petrol supply; and a full set of tools.

Solving the tool carrying problem

"The tool roll is carried in a container under the dash. The jack is mounted under the bonnet. The starting handle slips in a pocket on the near side, and the rest of the tools are carried under the rear squab. The difficult problem of stowing tools is solved without ugly excrescences on the running boards, which are free from any impedimenta.

"The price of the four-seater tested is £490, this being known as the Special model, which is the one we recommend. The standard car has canvas tyres, wood instead of steel wheels, and less luxurious equipment, and is painted in plain grey: its price is £450.

"In conclusion, we would say that this car can be recommended with confidence, and should appeal particularly to the family man who cannot afford the still larger 20hp model.

"Austin owners should note the very fine depot and service station at 479-83, Oxford Street. W. The service station is actually in Park Street, which runs parallel with Oxford Street. Work of every description can be carried out."

An Austin Twelve on the Exeter trial route

Three years following the Twelve-Four's launch, *The Autocar* decided that they would conduct a further road test, so over Christmas 1924 they drove one, fully laden, from London to Exeter and back, accompanying the trial. This is their report published on 9 January 1925:

"Five hundred miles is not a big proportion of the total distance covered yearly in motoring, but if the circumstances are particularly adverse and the route chosen for the run is difficult, an excellent idea can be obtained of the capability of a car.

Reasons for popularity

"The Austin Twelve is more than usually interesting, because it is one of the most popular machines of the present day and is appearing on the road in increasing numbers all over the Kingdom. Such popularity must be based on something which appeals particularly to the average motorist, and in the case of the Austin, one feature of this appeal is its modest price. Considering the equipment and finish, the car is really a tempting proposition, and if one adds to that the fact that it possesses a really good performance and is easy and pleasant to drive, the reason for its popularity becomes additionally clear.

"Part of our test included the London-Exeter-London Run, organised by the Motor Cycling Club and starting from Staines on Boxing night. The car was loaded with its full complement of four passengers, because a run of this nature should be undertaken with a full load normally carried by the ordinary motorist during a prolonged tour, and it may be mentioned, by the way, that the London-Exeter, though not a severe trial in the competition sense of the term, is considerably more exacting than a tour in ordinary circumstances.

Easy to handle

"Few cars, as good as they might be, could have performed better from any point of view. For one thing, the Austin is very easy to handle both as regards its steering and its gear change, two factors which make all the difference between the driver being tired out at the end of his 337-mile journey and finishing comparatively fresh. Another point, which is of equal importance, is that the seats, both front and rear, are particularly comfortable and have sufficient leg room. Those in the front are adjustable, which is a distinct advantage, and they are also provided with a much higher back than is frequently found, so that the passengers are comfortable the whole time.

"During the Exeter, a hurricane, reaching at times 50mph and popularly set down at 60mph, blew with tremendous violence and was accompanied by extremely heavy rain. The wind caused the car to swing out of its course every few minutes according to the increase or decrease of the successive gusts, and it is a great testimonial to the all-weather equipment which was in use almost for the entire distance, that at no time did the crew experience any actual discomfort from the rain, trying as circumstances might be in general. The only thing which might be noted was that the rigid side curtains were inclined to rattle, and do not admit so much light as do some of the latest types with narrow frames, whilst the rearmost curtain of all allowed water to creep between it and the hood in a gale such as the one experienced. On the other hand, the curtains are very easy to fit, and are properly housed in a compartment behind the rear seat in such a way that they can be got at with the minimum of trouble when required.

"As to the hood, the clips holding the forward crosspiece to the top of the windscreen are excellent; there is no fumbling for the catches, and it is easy to erect or lower the hood whilst while the car is running. Another point in its favour as affects protection from the weather is that the two-piece windscreen has a rubber strip between the upper and lower panels to prevent water being forced through by external wind pressure. As a whole, therefore, the car proved very comfortable, indeed, and kept its occupants quite dry.

Efficient lighting equipment

"Another thing which proved excellent was the lighting system, and though it may seem odd to comment on this point to-day when lighting systems are thought to be at a high pitch of perfection, yet it must be remembered that the call upon the accumulator during the London-Exeter is very high, and, in consequence, quite a number of cars have trouble with their lamps during the run, Now the point about the Austin installation is that the headlamps give what is really a magnificent light, far more than anyone would suspect could be possible without trial, while the side lights alone give a quite reasonable light for use in certain circumstances, and the tail light illuminates the number plate, which is more than some patterns do.

"The dynamo continues to charge when all the lamps are on; that is, it is keeping pace with the consumption of the current and putting a little back as well. At the end of the run the lamps were every bit as brilliant as they were at the commencement, in addition to which on the day following the run the car was left standing for two and a half hours outside a house with the side lamps and tail lamp on, and again there was no diminution of light.

Easy starting

"As the engine was started every time by its starting motor, even in the early morning, when it was stiff and the weather was cold, no fault can be found with the electric system generally. The engine is easy to start if careful use is made of the choke control for the carburettor first thing on a cold morning; the starting motor, although noisy in action, is quite certain on every occasion.

"At full throttle there is a degree of engine hardness, though this is not accompanied by any marked vibration, and some noise, yet one excellent point about the engine is that at anything up to three-quarter throttle it remains smooth and is quiet, which is the more important because nine-tenths of the work the car would have to do can be done without using full throttle. During our test, both on Marlpits and White Sheet Hills, there was a good bit of throttle in hand, and the car would respond to full throttle at once. The engine was not taken up any of these hills at full revs. as there was no need to do so. On Salcombe, one of the steepest of all the hills in the London-Exeter the engine even had something in hand, which is a good testimonial considering the load and the fact that the hood and curtains were up.

"It has been mentioned that the gear change is easy to handle, and so it is in ordinary touring work, the ratios and the slow movement when changing up being exactly fitted to the requirements of the average driver, but any man of experience or anyone handling the car on a very steep and long hill would wish for a clutch stop, as it is impossible to mesh the gears without a grating noise. A clutch stop would allow the change to be very quick, and would considerably lessen the work done by the engine as well as increase the speed of the car.

The four wheel brakes.

"It is obvious, however, that the Austin can tackle hills of, say, one in four, quite happily with four passengers. Considering the size of the body and, of course, as one must, the price of the car, there is ample speed, and one can say that 45mph over a measured mile would be about the correct maximum figure under full load. At all events, 30mph can be kept up for mile after mile, if necessary, quite smoothly and without fuss. Another interesting thing is that the top gear performance is good, and it is possible to drive comfortably in London traffic using this gear only, and to come down to a speed of about six or seven mph, and accelerate from there without difficulty.

"Great attraction to the car as a whole has resulted from the introduction of the four-wheel brake system now used, for though the brakes are not as powerful as they could be, and need distinct pressure to obtain the best results, yet they are smooth in action, they stop the car from skidding, and are infinitely better than the former rear brakes, besides needing far less attention. The concentration of the adjustment for all the brakes at one point is an admirable feature.

"The system, it will be remembered, is one where five drums are needed, the fifth being placed at the back of the gearbox with shoes which are controlled by the lever. This brake is very effective and rather fierce, its real use being demonstrated admirably by the stop and restart on White Sheet Hill, the ordinary pedal brakes being more than sufficient for everyday work. Though the lever is in the centre of the car, it is comfortably within the driver's reach at any time. On curves and corners the Austin holds the road very well, and the amount of inclination of the pivots gives just the right amount of castor return action after a corner.

"In its ordinary use 27mpg seems to be the correct petrol consumption. During the Exeter it naturally was lower and actually worked out at about 25mpg.

Excellence of details

"The Austin Twelve excels in its details. A rear screen is provided as an alternative to the rigid side curtains and is so contrived that it easily moves clear of the rear doors – there are four doors to the body – if used when the hood and side curtains are in place. In addition, it folds away in the back of the front seat, and is not unsightly in that position. In the instrument board are two cupboards, which are extremely useful, and pockets are formed in the upholstery on the sides of the doors which serve to hold maps or the detachable starting handle.

"The petrol tank filler is below the driver's seat and there is a tool kit housed out of the way in a special receptacle secured to the dash board and underneath the scuttle.

"In the engine compartment the oil level indicator and oil filler are both on the same side of the engine. The radiator can be drained easily, and oil can be removed from the base by unscrewing a large cap. All the minor bearings of the chassis are lubricated by grease gun. The magneto contact breaker is accessible, and fan adjustment easy.

"Incidentally, the engine keeps very cool, the radiator thermometer being up to normal heat on a cold day only when a long hill has been climbed, and only on one occasion was there any signs of boiling.

"Enough has been said to show why the Austin Twelve stands prominently in its class and to explain it popularity, for it is exactly the type of car which is most in demand to-day – a family carriage with a good and comfortable body, a sound performance and well equipped, a car that is easy to look after and inexpensive to run."

Data For The Driver

12hp, four cylinders, 72mm x 102mm (1660cc).
Annual road tax: £13.
Tested weight of complete car (less passengers):
    20cwt 1qtr 14 lbs [1036kg].
Weight per cc: 1.3 lbs [0.6kg].
Gear ratios: 20, 12, 8 and 5.18 to 1.
Spiral bevel final drive.
Half-elliptic front and rear springs.
765 x 105mm tyres on detachable steel wheels.
Wheelbase: 9ft 4in [2845mm].
Track: 4ft 4in [1321mm].
Fuel consumption: 25-27 mpg.
    [11.5 to 10.4 litres/100km].
Tank capacity: 8 gallons [36 litres].
Brakes on all four wheels.
Price: (four seater touring car) £355

Hill-climbing in Sydney

In 1927, on the other side of the world, the Australian motoring magazine *Motor Life* chose to re-examine the Austin Twelve, following the introduction of the more powerful long-stroke engine. The report, published in their edition of 18 June showed that they considered the new engine a vast improvement on the Austin Twelve's original power unit.

For the road test, *Motor Life* were provided with an Australian-bodied open tourer from the Sydney Austin dealership, Larke, Hoskins & Co. The car was not brand new as it had some 3000 miles on the clock having been a recent participant in the Royal Automobile Club of Australia's annual 10 day trials, following which the car had then been used as the agent's general runabout.

Three roads, Raglan Street, Balmoral Hill and David Street, all known for having steep hills and hairpin bends, were chosen for the road test.

The testers were generally impressed with the new long-stroke engine which they found to be livelier than its predecessor. They noted in their report that it ascended Raglan Street Hill in top gear right up to the last right hand bend when they had to change down to third, but still completed the climb at 21mph.

The rough and severe gradients encountered during their drive up Balmoral Hill, was accomplished only in second gear, as too did the run up David Street which had a gradient of 1 in 6, but a speed of 18 mph was recorded for the entire run.

The testers were generally very impressed with the Austin Twelve-Four, noting that it was an excellent example of the medium weight economical British car, and of the careful workmanship bestowed upon it during manufacture. On the flat they recorded a speed of 44mph in third gear, and 58 in top.

The Autocar tests a taxi

Both *The Motor* and *The Autocar* magazines have mostly devoted their road tests and subsequent reports to private motor cars, but in their edition published on 25 June 1937, *The Autocar* had taken the unusual step to test and report on the Austin Twelve-Four taxicab. The cab was loaned to them by Mann & Overton Ltd, and had just been delivered to them from the coach builder.

We all know them, the London taxicabs, and most of us sample them as "fares" at some time or other, but probably very few ordinary car owners indeed have ever driven a taxi. In any case, it is not the kind of vehicle most are likely to be anxious to try for pleasure, and in the nature of things the opportunity is virtually non-existent.

It was suggested that it would be interesting to take one out on test in exactly the same manner as applies to the cars tested by *The Autocar*. A natural thought was an Austin cab, of which there are so many on the London streets – in fact, it is now the most popular make of taxi in the Metropolitan area.

The vehicle provided was a brand new one, which apparently had done no more mileage than is represented by the run down from the Birmingham factory, and it was only distinguished from the normal taxi plying for hire by the absence of a "clock" and of the special Scotland Yard number plate on the rear.

Looking down onto the bonnet

"One was prepared for some striking impressions compared with a car, and straight away the point that seemed so different was sitting high-up, with the steering column not far off the vertical and the pedals almost immediately under one's feet, together with the extraordinary range of driving vision this position affords. There is the effect of looking down onto the bonnet and wings, both of which are fully visible. It is realised at once why taxi drivers are able to put their vehicles through apparently impossible spaces and to drive confidently within inches of other vehicles. At once a stranger finds himself able to begin emulating their example in these matters without claiming fully professional techniques and proficiency!

"Of course the taxi is essentially a town vehicle, which spends the greater part of its life at speeds under 30mph, and its whole design is to that end. On this occasion, not only was the vehicle handled in town traffic for a considerable distance in the sum total, in conditions corresponding to its normal operating, but it was also taken into the country, and even onto Brooklands track where, to say the least, it created no small stir. In town it is as handy a vehicle as can be imagined, with the excellent driving vision already mentioned and the first rate manoeuvrability. There is certainly nothing violent about the acceleration, yet because of these other points, it can get from one place to another in and around London about as quickly as anything else.

"The 12.8hp four-cylinder engine is a notably sturdy and hard pulling unit, on the lines of the type used in the old Heavy Twelve Austin car. Top gear ratio feels lower than it is, especially when speed is increased out on the open road. The lower gears are used only to get moving, and, though the vehicle will start on second, to use first to move off seems better. Incidentally, a cab driver – among several who became interested in this "pirate" and wanted to know what it was doing – said that a considerable

The taxi managed a restart on the 1-4 gradient test hill at Brooklands.

number of his colleagues start on second gear, and probably would not be able to make a quiet change from first to second.

What price cold weather?

"Actually it is not worth using first above about 6mph or even third beyond about 25. In neutral the gear lever is almost vertical, admirably placed for changing, and there is synchromesh on third and top. The other gears require normal double-clutching treatment, but the change up from second to third is assisted by the synchromesh.

"It must be a breezy and not too pleasant occupation driving a taxi in cold weather, for with the entirely open left-hand side of the driving compartment and the absence of any protection above the door on the right, wind and draught blow straight through, as must the rain, too. I imagine. Apparently, this bleakness is an outcome of official regulations.

"Judged by main-road use, the vehicle is noisy anywhere around 40mph, the engine then appearing to be doing a good deal of work, though it keeps at it without any signs of distress. Performance of a high order is not expected, and really the vehicle can be got along outside town in a rather surprising manner. One is not supposed to maintain 45mph on a taxi, certainly not so in the opinion of most car drivers who were overtaken in the process, some of whom seemed to be mystified, not to say annoyed, at the spectacle of a cab in full flight!

"Up the usual 1 in 6½ hill used in the road tests is made a sure, if not spectacular, climb in second gear at 10mph. In its slow but certain manner it also scaled the Brooklands Test Hill, and would get away on the 1 in 4 section of that gradient if the engine was revved up enough, though not liking it very much. The timed quarter-mile at Brooklands was amusing, the vehicle hardly appearing to be moving on the great expanse of concrete, but the speedometer nobly going round to 53-54 with the wind.

"A taxi is quite heavy, carrying some 28cwt, with an engine rated at 12.8hp and under 2 litres capacity. This weight probably helps with regards sitting down on the road, for it handles rather well, even at fast speeds, provided that nothing too exuberant in the way of cornering is attempted, where there is apt to be a top-heavy suggestion.

"Steering must obviously be a very important matter, and a good compromise has been struck between lightness and heaviness, so that the steering stays firm. One knows exactly where one is with it, and it doesn't require too much effort for turning round. The ratio is quite moderate, 2⅓ turns of the wheel being required from lock to lock. That brings up one of the outstanding points of a taxi, the smallness of the turning circle. To turn round you put the wheel hard over, and there is almost the effect of the nose swinging on a pivot.

"Everything about the vehicle is of good quality and

The Austin Taxi parked next to a 1937 Lagonda sports tourer at Brooklands (Photo from The Autocar)

solid, obviously made to last and to give the minimum of trouble, for here, more than most cars, trouble means money. The main seating compartment is well done, with durable leather upholstery and good fittings and the doors shut in the true coach built manner. In front there is more than the average amount of metalwork and a considerable sympathetic vibration is set up somewhere here at any appreciable speed.

"Instruments include the necessary gauges – oil pressure, ammeter and petrol, and a separately mounted speedometer in full view of the driver, set out at an angle from the board so that it shall be really clear to see. This instrument is purely a speedometer, with no mileage recorders, and is permanently illuminated in conjunction with the ignition switch. It proved to be within 0.75mph of accuracy at the all-important 30 and 34mph, fast at 50, a speed which presumably few taxicab drivers ever see on their vehicles. The brakes did not give as good a test figure as would have been expected but probably, in view of the extreme newness, were bedding down and would have benefitted from adjustment.

"Always of course, taxicabs have been hedged about by a mass of regulations which call for this and that feature, and, again, are subject to periodical police inspection and passing out for condition. One result is the provision of a bulb horn (to sound which effectively is quite an art in itself these days!), no electric horn being allowed. It is a not unamusing point, bearing on the very rare cases of the failure of horns on our cars, that this bulb horn somewhat departed from grace. It did not give out, but started to produce an odd sort of note, probably needing adjustment of the reed.

"A capital point is the provision of a twin-blade windscreen wiper which sweeps across the whole width of glass in a horizontal plane. The screen is divided, to open. This was a Trico suction wiper, and had a reserve tank under the bonnet to prevent immediate 'drying up' when accelerating. Fuel feed is by an Autovac, now practically unknown on private cars, and a little point noticed in connection with the fuel system is a neatly labelled push-and-pull tap on the outside of the body to cut off the supply to the carburettor – apparently another official requirement, The tank is amidships and the filler at the side. The engine starts easily and is notable for a particularly slow and quiet tick-over, which clearly is a point of importance. Also, this engine will pull steadily on top gear at 9 to 10mph.

"It is of interest that there are now more than 5000 Austin taxi-cabs registered in the Metropolitan area, of a total of approximately 8000. This run was arranged in conjunction with the Austin Motor Co. Ltd., by the distributors in London for the Austin taxicab, Mann & Overton Ltd., 177, Battersea Bridge Road, SW11.

"Contrast is the essence of testing work, but I wonder how many people have handled in the same day a taxicab and an 85mph sports car. That happened in my case during this special test. I hope the taxi turns out to be a good one in its future owner's hands – it should be nicely run-in by now! – and I wonder, too, if it will ever find itself at Brooklands again in its long career of public life.

"Rather disappointingly, I wasn't hailed once, which was somewhat surprising during the recent bus strike, but then I didn't venture into the West End. I did, however, manage to "leg-pull" a colleague who was coming out of Waterloo Station and, naturally enough, failed to spot me. His reply to my "Taxi Sir" was a solemn shake of the head, and he was continuing on his leisurely way when, as he said afterwards, something familiar in the voice from a taxi registered and he took another casual look, recognised me, and rapidly sorted things out-to the considerable amusement of both of us, but no financial benefit to me! H.S.E."

In *The Motor* during war-time

Finally, in No 32 of a series of articles entitled "In Their Day", *The Motor* took a look at the Austin Twelve. As this article was published on 13 October 1943, one would have thought that at that particular time, *The Motor* would had had more appropriate subjects to write about, but their review must have been of interest 21 years after the Twelve-Four was first put on the market, and during the war both magazines had regular nostalgic features looking back to happier days.

Some cars have inspired awe, some enthusiasm, and some downright affection, but none, with the possible exception of the Austin Seven, has inspired so much affection as the heavy Austin Twelve, and few cars have had a longer innings. Introduced in 1922, the Austin Twelve chassis has always been famous for its sturdiness – almost a byword, in fact – and the very pattern of solid British virtues. Built for long life, the car was modelled very much upon the Austin Twenty and amusingly, by modern standards, was referred to as the "Light Austin".

Appealed to the owner driver

Light or not, the Austin Twelve was aimed at a definite public – particularly the people living away from the big towns, whether farmers or country gentlemen. At a time when country garages were infrequent and ill-staffed, The Austin Twelve appealed particularly to the owner-driver. The chassis itself was a straight forward job with semi elliptic springs all round, braced together firmly at the front by a solidly mounted engine and gearbox unit which drove, via a fabric universal, a spiral bevel final drive in a semi-floating back axle. To assist amateur overhauling the four-cylinder 72 by 102 side-valve engine had a detachable head, and when many slow-revving engines still depended on splash lubrication, the Twelve employed a pressure system with an oil gauge on the dash.

Few cars can have been easier to drive: a single dry plate clutch transmitted the power so smoothly that the car would move away on its top gear of 5.2 with very little clutch slip, and the gear change itself, operated by a central ball change lever, was very simple. [Note: the ball change superseded the gate change in late 1928]. The four-speed gearbox, rather a rarity in the early twenties, could scarcely have been easier to use, although the change was probably one of the most leisurely to be found. In bottom gear the car could surmount almost any hill, which made it popular to the farming community, whilst in top gear the speed range was from a brisk walking pace to just under 45mph, which was the car's maximum speed. With a full load of five passengers the Austin would pick up well in top gear from low speeds, whilst a fine suspension, good upholstery and high backs of the seats, both front and rear, made it most popular not only with the owner-driver but with the passengers.

The body most usually fitted in the early days was a long four to five-seater tourer, with what was euphemistically known at the time as a one-man hood. The windscreen was a two-piece device, in which the upper panel was hinged at the top and the lower panel at the bottom, so that the needs of the driver in those wiper-less years were catered for in sun, rain and fog. [Note: the hinged bottom panel of the windscreen was not a feature which lasted very long, and was soon replaced with a fixed panel]. The back passengers were kept warm by an additional windscreen, which folded away neatly behind the front seats, and side curtains would keep out the weather when the hood was up.

In the event of a breakdown or roadside punctures the driver would find the spare wheel at the back of the car, where it was stowed to avoid cluttering the running boards and obstructing the doors, whilst the tools, including the jack and wheel brace, were all put away in convenient lockers or clip holders.

The unusual petrol tank position.

It may seem odd to find the petrol tank slung beneath the sliding front seat between the propeller shaft and the side member of the frame; but it must be remembered that with the normal petrol consumption of 30mpg, the eight gallon tank would give the car a range of 240 miles, while people did not, as a rule, drive so far in 1922 as they do now. Furthermore, there were no petrol pumps in those days, so filling up an external tank from cans was liable to remove the paint and varnish of the pre-cellulose finish. An Autovac delivered the fuel from the tank to the single carburettor.

If the Austin Twelve was designed to last there was certainly no delay into putting in to production. The first chassis was on the road developing 20bhp and running over a speed range of seven to 45mph in top gear within three months of the design being sanctioned. The first examples were on sale in 1922, and the Austin Twelve with only minor developments, including a longer stroke engine, continued an unbroken production run of 12 years. The engine, moreover, is still made, and forms the power unit of many London taxicabs.

Besides the tourer, the cars were also supplied as two seater, coupé and saloon models, as well as with special bodies by a variety of coachbuilders. The prices ranged from £550 for the tourer in 1922 to £265 in 1934 and £275 for a fabric saloon in 1931.

Editor's note:

The Austn Twelve-Four was launched in the autumn of 1921, but *not,* as one might have expected, at the London Motor Show, which was held during that year at both Olympia (Kensington) and White City (Shepherds Bush), but at the Austin Motor Company's main London showroom in Oxford Street. The reason being that as the Austin Motor Company was still in receivership, they were banned by the Society of Motor Manufacturer and Traders (SMMT) from exhibiting there. The first Austin Twelve was purchased on 1 January 1922.

Chapter Three

HOW THEY WERE MADE

This chapter takes a look at how The Austin Motor Company manufactured their motor cars in the 1920s, and in particular the Austin Twelve-Four.

Up until the First World War, the methods used in the manufacturing of motor cars was still very much based upon those used during the building of horse-drawn vehicles, that is to say they were generally all hand built to individual requirements.

In the United States of America, motor manufacturers had already installed production lines in order to be able to turn out large quantities of motor cars in the shortest possible time, using the least number of employees At Henry Ford's invitation, Herbert Austin was able to see at first-hand how the Ford Motor Company in Detroit were turning out their Model T motor cars in such large quantities, and on his return to the UK he set about installing something similar at Longbridge.

By 1926 Longbridge had become fully converted to mass production but in doing so still ensured that each motor car was built with the finest materials available and finished to the highest of standards in order that the purchaser was provided with a quality product that would give him or her many years of trouble-free motoring.

The graphic illustration drawn by GH Davis featured on pages 36-37 was published as a centre spread in *The Illustrated London News* for 15 June 1926, and clearly shows in diagrammatic form the processes involved in manufacturing Austin motor cars. By the mid-1920s The Austin Motor Company had adopted mass production and had sophisticated assembly lines in place to aid production as can clearly be seen in the illustration.

The text from this centre spread reads as follows:

"The modern British automobile has now become such a reliable vehicle that it is wonderful to examine, at one of the great motor works in the country, the production of a car from the first to the final operation, and see how thoroughly it is all done, and what an incredibly short space of time is occupied.

"In the diagrammatic drawing *(made in the Austin Motor Company's Longbridge Works at Birmingham)* it was of course impossible to show the actual making of all the parts large and small, from the smallest screw to the engine and gearbox, but we have depicted in the smaller illustrations just a few of the methods of testing during the manufacture of these parts, and two of the tools that are used.

"The balancing of the crankshaft for example, must be dead true because of the vibrations caused by out-of-balance masses rotating at high speeds. A mass of engine ounce in weight revolving in a circle of twelve inches at 4000 revolutions per minute will give rise to an outward pull of centrifugal force amounting to 86 lbs. Thus the new Gisholt balancing machine, shown in one of our illustrations is a very useful and necessary test.

"Another of the smaller illustrations shows how the light saloon bodies are now rapidly constructed of light metals such as aluminium yet are capable of withstanding hard use on the road and are free from drumming. For now that the totally enclosed body is so popular in this country, and when hesitation drives the majority of modern motorists to use the small car, lightness must go hand in hand with strength, otherwise the wonderful little lines will be overburdened.

"In the centre diagrammatic drawing we see the whole operation of assembling the parts which have been manufactured somewhere in the works or by other firms specialising in such components: so that, by following the large numbers from one to twenty the series of operations is made clear, from the moment the pressed chassis frame is placed into position to the time when the finished gleaming car glides silently and smoothly from its birthplace to be delivered to the purchaser. We see it being pushed on from one gang of men to another down the rails, taking shape as it goes. Part after part being rapidly fixed into position until it takes its first taste of the open road, minus body and is put into the hands of the expert tester.

"Then, when it comes back again the body is waiting slung to its overhead rail ready to be dropped into position. Very soon body and chassis are connected. Sundries have been added and the car goes out again for another test. It is sent roaring up the test hill with a gradient of one in 5.1, round the private test track at the works, and then out and onto the open road. After all has been reported as O.K. it is finally passed out of the works ready for use. Truly the modern British motor car is second to none in the world."

The timber framework in the process of being manufactured from well-seasoned ash. (Photo: Barry Davies)

Panel beaters forming the body sections which will go to provide the Windsor Saloon bodies. (Photo: Barry Davies)

The large double-page spread showing how the Austin Twelve-Four is manufactured. (Illustration from The Illustrated London News*)*

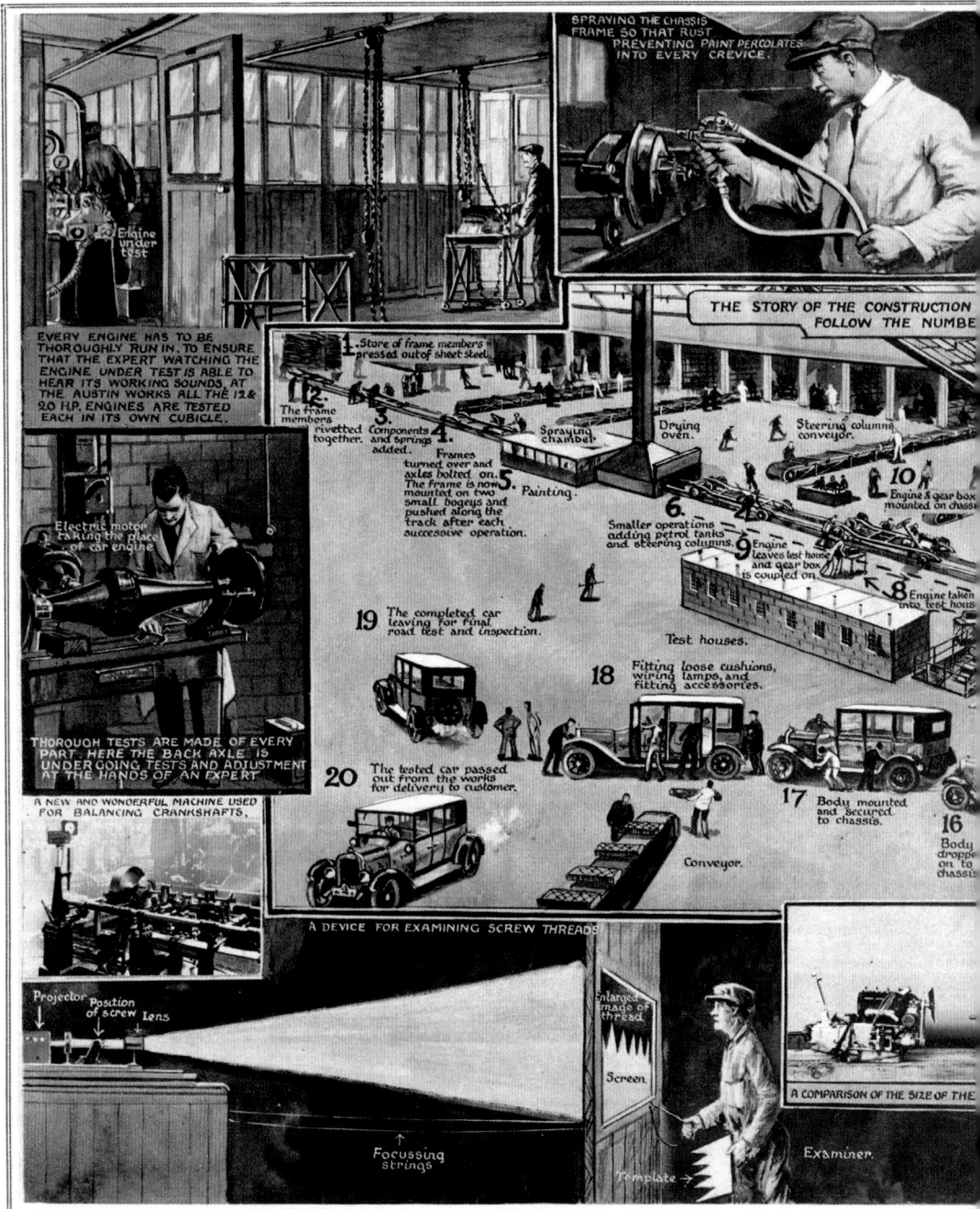

WHICH BRITISH MANUFACTURE IS UNSURPASSED.

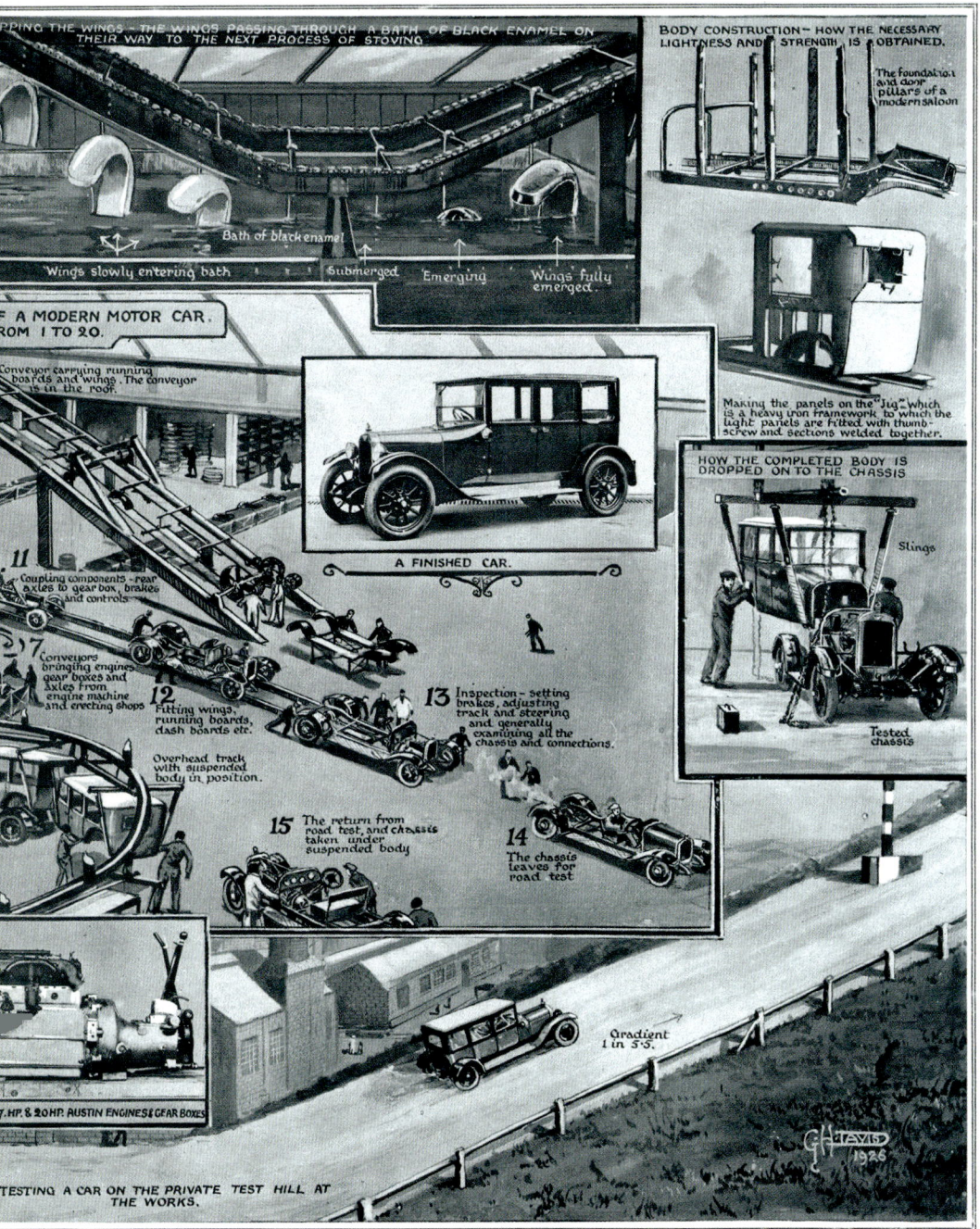

AND ASSEMBLAGE OF A CAR IN ONE OF THE GREAT BRITISH MOTOR-WORKS.

…axation drives the majority of modern motorists to use the small car, lightness must go hand-in-hand with strength, otherwise the wonderful little engines will be overburdened. In the centre diagrammatic drawing we see the whole operation of assembling the parts, which have been manufactured elsewhere in the works or by other firms specialising in a certain component; so that, by following the large numbers from one to twenty, the series of operations is made clear, from the moment when the pressed chassis frame is placed in position, to the time when the gleaming finished car glides silently and smoothly from its birthplace to be delivered to the purchaser. We see it being pushed on from one gang of men to another down the steel rails, taking shape as it goes, part after part being rapidly fixed in position, until it takes its first taste of the open road, minus body, and in the hands of the expert tester. Then, when it comes back again, the body is waiting, slung to its overhead rail, ready to be dropped into position; and soon body and chassis are connected, sundries have been added, and the car goes out again for another test. It is sent roaring up the test hill of a gradient of one in 5.1, round the private test-track at the works, and then out on to the open road. After all has been reported as O.K., it is finally passed out of the works ready for use. Truly the modern British motor-car is second to none in the world.

Craftsmen working on the rear section of the open tourers. (Photo: Barry Davies)

Construction of bodies, probably for the Austin Twenty, in the West Works in 1921. (Photo: Barry Davies)

Washing of the Twelve-Four engine blocks. (Photo: Duncan Lye)

Completed engines en route to be installed in their chassis. (Photo: Duncan Lye)

Automatic nickel-plating of radiator shells. (Photo: Duncan Lye)

Spray painting radiator cores. (Photo: Duncan Lye)

HOW THEY WERE MADE

...WHICH BRITISH MANUFACTURE IS UNSURPASSED.

ARTIST, G. H. DAVIS. (COPYRIGHTED.)

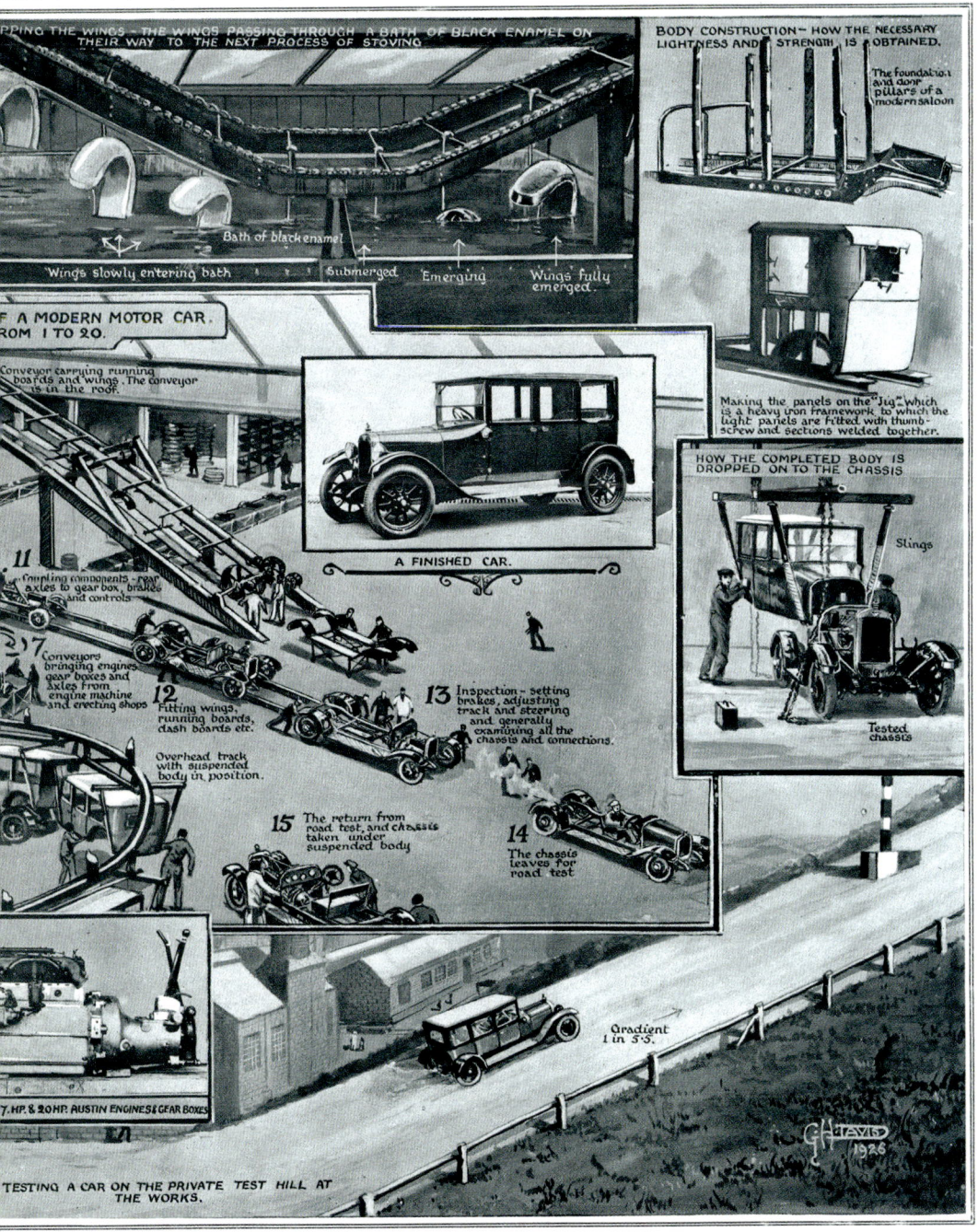

...AND ASSEMBLAGE OF A CAR IN ONE OF THE GREAT BRITISH MOTOR-WORKS.

...axation drives the majority of modern motorists to use the small car, lightness must go hand-in-hand with strength, otherwise the wonderful little ...ngines will be overburdened. In the centre diagrammatic drawing we see the whole operation of assembling the parts, which have been manufactured ...lsewhere in the works or by other firms specialising in a certain component; so that, by following the large numbers from one to twenty, the series ...f operations is made clear, from the moment when the pressed chassis frame is placed in position, to the time when the gleaming finished car glides ...ilently and smoothly from its birthplace to be delivered to the purchaser. We see it being pushed on from one gang of men to another down the ...teel rails, taking shape as it goes, part after part being rapidly fixed in position, until it takes its first taste of the open road, minus body, and in ...he hands of the expert tester. Then, when it comes back again, the body is waiting, slung to its overhead rail, ready to be dropped into position; ...nd soon body and chassis are connected, sundries have been added, and the car goes out again for another test. It is sent roaring up the test hill ...f a gradient of one in 5.1, round the private test-track at the works, and then out on to the open road. After all has been reported as O.K., it is ...nally passed out of the works ready for use. Truly the modern British motor-car is second to none in the world.

Craftsmen working on the rear section of the open tourers. (Photo: Barry Davies)

Construction of bodies, probably for the Austin Twenty, in the West Works in 1921. (Photo: Barry Davies)

Washing of the Twelve-Four engine blocks. (Photo: Duncan Lye)

Completed engines en route to be installed in their chassis. (Photo: Duncan Lye)

Automatic nickel-plating of radiator shells. (Photo: Duncan Lye)

Spray painting radiator cores. (Photo: Duncan Lye)

HOW THEY WERE MADE

Degreasing and cleaning saloon bodies prior to painting. (Photo from The Austin Magazine*)*

Sixteen-Six chassis on the production line circa 1929. (Compare this photo with the illustration shown on the cigarette card in chapter 7.)

A Burnham body being lowered into place on a Sixteen-Six chassis. (Photo from The Austin Magazine*)*

A line of completed Sixteen-Six Burnham saloons receiving a final inspection, circa 1929. (Photo: The Vintage Austin Register Archive)

An impressive line-up of completed cars and chassis ready to be shipped off to the dealerships, or in the case of the chassis, to Australia, New Zealand, or UK-based coachbuilders such as Mulliner, Hoyal or Gordon; circa 1928. (Photo: the Vintage Austin Register Archive)

39

Chapter Four

THE STANDARD AUSTIN BODY STYLES FROM THE LONGBRIDGE FACTORY

During the thirteen years when the Austin Twelve-Four was produced, the Company came up with 25 different names for the various styles of coachwork that were available. Probably the best remembered names are the Clifton tourer, with 30,441 produced, the Windsor saloon 18,013 (this figure includes Burnham production for 1929), and the Burnham Saloon (5792, except 1929). To support this, it is these three particular models which have the highest survival rate out of all of those originally offered.

The fabric saloons were among those not given a name until 1930 when names such as Beaconsfield, Marlow, Salisbury, Watford, and Wycombe were introduced, but by then the novelty of owning a fabric bodied motor car was beginning to fade and within a year, they completely disappeared from the sales brochures.

How the Company decided on the various names will probably never be known, but as we can see from the following, they included areas within the United Kingdom which were perhaps considered relatively affluent, such as Hertford, Salisbury and Westminster, and the Company even included the two prestigious public schools, Harrow and Eton.

It has been suggested that a few names of Buckinghamshire towns were selected because of the railway stations from which Sir Herbert would disembark in order to meet up with a certain lady friend who happened to live in Iver. But to be fair, there is no evidence to support this claim. It should be remembered that Herbert was born in the Buckinghamshire village of Little Missenden, although he was just four years of age when the family moved to Yorkshire.

The various models are listed in alphabetical order and are shown in original illustrations from relevant brochures, together with photographs of surviving examples. As the years progressed from 1928 onwards, we find that Twelve-Four bodies could be fitted on the six-cylinder 15.9hp chassis which had the same wheelbase, and where there were no pictures or

The Beaconsfield fabric saloon in black, an illustration from the 1931 model year catalogue.

illustrations of the Twelve-Four version available, those with the Sixteen-Six engine have been substituted, because other than the Sixteen-Six having wire wheels and louvered bonnet sides, the coachwork was identical. As a matter of interest, the Sixteen-Six, or Sixteen Light-Six, was introduced at the 1927 Motor Show at first it was simply a Windsor saloon fitted with the larger engine, but when it went into production in March 1928, it was listed as the Burnham.

Beaconsfield Four-Light Fabric Saloon – October 1930 to 1931

The Beaconsfield was one of four body styles introduced in October 1930, which were the last of the fabric bodied saloons offered by the Company. The other three were the Marlow, the Salisbury, and the Wycombe. The Beaconsfield and the Marlow followed the design from the Watford which had been introduced a few months earlier; the Salisbury and the Wycombe were six-light saloons. Strictly speaking the Beaconsfield was the name for this body on the Sixteen-Six chassis, it was called the Marlow on the Twelve-Four chassis.

Berkeley Saloon – October 1932 to 1934

The Berkeley Saloon and the Berkeley Saloon De Luxe were introduced for the 1933 model year, and were the first to be manufactured on the new cross braced drop frame chassis, with synchromesh gearbox and the new style Magna wheels. The windscreen and door pillars were slightly inclined. The doors continued down to the level of the running board. The Berkeley De Luxe had picnic tables, arm rests, bumpers, and a sunroof; it was also available on the 16hp chassis. The short-lived 1935 model had doors rather than louvres in the bonnet sides.

Berkeley Single Landaulet – 1923 to 1927

The Berkeley Single Landaulet was offered very early on in the life of the Twelve-Four, and is certainly a throw-back to the Edwardian days when it was normal to engage the services of a chauffeur to drive your motor car. The description in the sales brochure makes it quite clear that this particular model was intended to be driven by a chauffeur. Seating in the rear was intended for just two people, whilst provision was made for two additional passengers who would have sat on folding down seats attached to the rear of the partition. There were only 197 Berkeley Single Landaulets manufactured and they were discontinued in 1927. The price was £525.

Seeing how similar this model was to the later taxicabs, it is possible that William Overton launched

Above: The Berkeley De Luxe saloon in black, an illustration from the 1934 model year catalogue.

Left: The 1930 Beaconsfield is actually a Sixteen-Six, but the style of coachwork was identical to the Twelve-Four Marlow. This is the only known survivor.
(Photo: Michael Flack)

A 1934-35 model Berkeley Saloon; note doors in bonnet sides. (Owner unknown; photo from author's collection or Vintage Austin Register Archive)

Below: Catalogue illustration of Berkeley single landaulet.

Above: Catalogue illustration of the original Burnham saloon made from 1928 to 1930; this is a Sixteen-Six.

Right: Paddy McKendry's 1929 Burnham Saloon. (Photo: David Heatley)

Below right: 1930 Burnham Saloon owned by H Kelly, taken at the Ulster Festival of Steam.

Below: 1929 Burnham Saloon. (Photo: K Wright)

a small fleet of these to work as taxicabs in and around Manchester, and which, on being greatly approved by the Manchester "cabbies" led him to approach Austin to consider changes to the chassis which would make them suitable for use in London (see chapter 8 on taxicabs). At the time of writing there are no known survivors.

Burnham Saloon – August 1928 to October 1932

Towards the latter part of the 1920s the Company's flagship saloon, the Windsor, was considered to be dated-looking and therefore needed to be replaced with something more up to date. The Burnham was introduced on the new Sixteen-Six chassis but also became available on the Twelve-Four chassis in August 1928 as a 1929 model. It was a handsome looking motor car which, like its predecessor, won considerable approval from the buying public, and as such many fine examples are still providing good reliable service today. It originally cost £320. It was also available with a division but then changed its name to Iver, the same name which had been used for the Windsor with division. In August 1930 the Burnham design was brought up-to-date, with a bit more curvature to the roof and rear quarters.

Carlton Saloon – September 1933 to 1934

The Carlton name had been used for an Austin Twenty saloon until 1932. It was used again for this five-seven seater saloon introduced for the Twelve-Four and Sixteen-Six in September 1933, mounted on the new long-wheelbase (10ft) chassis. Clearly it was intended mainly for the six-cylinder model but was also available with the 12.8hp engine, which sold for £305. A version of the Carlton was available with a partition and called Iver, see below. The 1935 models had doors rather than louvres in the bonnet sides but were soon replaced by the York and Chalfont.

Chalfont Saloon – 1934 to 1935

This was the name for the new long-wheelbase York with a cowled radiator when it was fitted with a division, and replaced the last of the Ivers. It is not certain whether any were built on the Twelve-Four chassis.

Clifton Tourer – 1922 to June 1930

The Clifton Tourer, or the five-seater touring car as it was known when launched in 1922, is without a doubt

Far left: The Carlton saloon in red, an illustration from the 1934 model year catalogue.

Left: This 1934 Carlton is a Sixteen version, but the coachwork is exactly the same as that fitted to the Twelve-Four chassis. Note doors in the bonnet sides. (Photo: Alan Milliner)

one of the most aesthetically pleasing models within the Twelve-Four range. Its well-designed lines go in and out in all the right places, making this a delightful example of Longbridge design. We are fortunate that due to its popularity and robust construction many superb examples are still around today, but regrettably only a very few of those can be included in this book. The example shown above would have cost £295. This is the original Clifton with narrow doors and loop-type door handles. In the catalogue issued in June 1928, there was a new style Clifton, looking much more like the Open Road with wide doors and T-type handles, but still having its own design of hood and side screens. This lasted until about June 1930.

Catalogue illustration of Clifton tourer.

The earliest known open touring car of 1922. Tony Smallbone with Vintage Austin Register founder member the late RJ (Bob) Wyatt MBE. (Photo: Tony Smallbone)

"Old Min" the red 1930 Clifton tourer which was at one time owned by Spike Milligan and Peter Sellers. (Photo: C Williams)

Two photos of a 1924 open tourer, the model which only got the Clifton name later. (Photo: Tony Smallbone)

Below: A pair of 1928 Clifton tourers owned by Messrs Davis and Eggenton. (Photo: Michael Eggenton)

Eton Two-Seater – late 1929 without a name, then from October 1930 to 1931

This body style had been introduced in 1929 at first without a name (see two-seater below). For the 1931 season when Austin introduced more model names, it became the Eton on the Twelve-Four chassis, and the Harrow on the Sixteen-Six chassis, named after two of England's premier schools. The Eton now cost £275. The name lasted only a year for the two-seater body on the Twelve-Four chassis which later adopted the Harrow name already used on the Sixteen-Six.

THE STANDARD AUSTIN BODY STYLES

Far left: The Eton Two-Seater in yellow, an illustration from the 1931 model year catalogue.

Left: This 1930 Eton was originally marketed as the two-seater. (Photo: R Long)

The Eton name was then used for the two-seater body found on the 12/6 and the Light 12/4 (11.9hp) chassis.

Fabric Four-Light Saloon – 1928 to 1930

The fabric saloon was inspired by the methods used during the First World War for stretching the fabric covering over the wooden framework of fighter aeroplanes. The method was later perfected by Weymann for use on motor cars which, it was claimed, helped to reduce the weight and prevented rattles. However, they were prone to damage which proved difficult to repair. Austin-built fabric saloons were discontinued in 1931. The four-light version as can be seen was fitted with dummy hood irons in place of the rear quarter-lights of the six-light version. The De Luxe version was available with Triplex safety glass all round and cost £325. The image shown is of the 15.9hp version.

Catalogue illustration of fabric four-light saloon.

Fabric Six-Light Saloon – 1927 to 1930

This was the first catalogued Austin body style to feature fabric construction, as it appeared in late 1927. Apart from the fact that this model has six windows instead of the four, it is identical to the four-light version shown above. This image is again of the Sixteen-Six (15.9hp) version as can be determined from the wire wheels and louvered bonnet sides. Wire wheels could be fitted on the Twelve-Four for an additional charge of £10. The price in 1929 for this car was £315 or £340 for the De Luxe version which was fitted with Triplex glass for all windows.

Two photos of the same fabric four-light saloon 90 years apart. The top photograph shows the car when quite new. The photograph below is the same car after being neglected for 90 years. It is currently undergoing restoration.

Harley All Weather Coupé – 1922 to 1925

An early addition to the Austin Twelve-Four range of models which was introduced in 1922 along with the tourer and the two-four seater – all of which were unnamed at that stage. The Harley was perhaps so named to appeal to medical doctors as it was considered that members of that profession would appreciate a lighter version of the 20hp models for their daily rounds. The price in 1924 was £525. The Harley was discontinued in 1925. The name was later revived for the saloon body on the 12/6 chassis in 1931.

And what it should look like once restored! (Photo: John Bedford)

45

Right: Catalogue illustration of fabric six-light saloon, this is a Sixteen-Six.
Far right: The 1929 Twelve-Four six-light fabric bodied saloon. (Photo from author's collection or Vintage Austin Register Archive)

Right: Catalogue illustration of Harley All-Weather Coupé.

Far right: A surviving 1924 Harley All Weather Coupé (Photo: Brian Parker)

Above: The Harrow Two-four seater in red, an illustration from the 1934 model year catalogue.

Above right: 1934 Harrow Two-four seater, with doors rather than louvres in the bonnet sides. (Owner and picture source unknown)

Harrow Two-Four Seater – 1931 to 1934

The identical twin to the Eton, to which it presents a remarkable likeness. In fact they were basically the same body but when the names were introduced in 1931, Eton was the name for this body on the Twelve-Four chassis, and Harrow was the name when it was fitted to the Sixteen-Six chassis. For the 1932 model year, Austin did not include a two-seater on the Twelve chassis in their catalogue, and when the body style came back for the 1933 Twelve, it too adopted the Harrow name, which was then used for two model years through 1934. The Eton name survived for two-seater bodies on the 12/6 and Light 12/4 chassis.

Hertford Two-Four Seater – 1922 to 1926

This was the third model in the range when the Twelve-Four was introduced in 1922, but was originally unnamed the Hertford name was adopted for the 1925 season. The Hertford, it was claimed, was a two-four seater, but behind the adjustable front seats there was enough room to accommodate two further passengers on what was described as "detachable auxiliaries". When removed, the space could be used for luggage. Additionally there was the dickey seat which offered accommodation for two more passengers. For some reason, there was no two-four seater in the 1927 catalogue, and the 1928 two-seater did not have a name.

Hertford Six-Light Saloon – 1934 to 1935

The Hertford name was revived in late 1934 for a six-light saloon with cowled radiator on the short wheelbase chassis (9ft 4in); otherwise it was similar to the York. It replaced the Berkeley and over 600 Twelve-Fours were made in 1935. It was also available on the 16/18hp chassis.

THE STANDARD AUSTIN BODY STYLES

Far left: Catalogue illustration of the Hertford Two-four seater.

Left: A 1924 Hertford Two-four seater. (Photo: Brian Parker)

The Hertford saloon in red, an illustration from the 1935 model year catalogue.

Iver Saloon with Division – 1927 to 1934

The Iver is one of the more confusing model names in the Twelve-Four range since it was used for four very different body styles, the only common feature being that they all had a glass division between the front and rear seats. The first Iver was based on the Windsor saloon and was added to the range in 1927 when it cost £405. Next came an Iver based on the Burnham, offered from October 1928 to 1932, and this was followed by a short-lived model based on the Berkeley. The final Iver was based on the new long-wheelbase Carlton saloon in October 1933; it could be fitted with occasional seats as an option, and cost £315. It lasted little more than a year, and when the Carlton was replaced by the York long-wheelbase model for the 1935 model year, the version with a division was named the Chalfont.

Marlow Four-Light Fabric Saloon – 1930 to 1931

The Marlow was, and still is something of a mystery motor car, as in addition to there being no known survivors there are also no known photographs to indicate just what it looked like. The 1931 model year brochure of 1930 suggests that it is similar to the Wycombe, which had six windows and was offered at the same price. In fact it seems likely that the Marlow had the same body as the Beaconsfield Sixteen-Six, and the Watford Twelve-Four. It was in production for about one year from 1930 to 1931, and was priced at £299.

Evidence that the Marlow existed can be found in the two following newspaper adverts. In *The Yorkshire Post* for Saturday 31 January 1931, the Central Garage, Bradford was offering a new Austin 12hp Marlow saloon four-light fabric saloon, with all black fabric and red leather seats for £299. Just a few years later, in *The Evening Sentinel* newspaper for Wednesday 7 April 1937, Olympia Motors of Elder Road, Cobridge advertised an Austin Twelve-Four Heavy Marlow Saloon, a good reliable car for sale for just £30,

"New" Windsor Saloon – 1931 to 1932

With the popularity of the Windsor name, Longbridge was reluctant to dispense with it entirely, but it seems

Above: Catalogue illustration of the original Iver saloon of 1927 with division.

Left: Two photos of the interior of a 1927 Iver (Photo: Peter Wright)

The New Windsor saloon in blue, an illustration from the 1932 model year catalogue.

1931-32 New Windsor Saloon. (Photo: Jodi Kaldenberg)

to have been brought back only for the 1932 model year when the catalogue listed a "New" Windsor body on both the Sixteen-Six and Twelve-Four chassis. It looked like the second type Burnham, but could be distinguished by a belt moulding. More importantly, the coachwork was of pressed steel, presumably without the traditional wooden frame, and the Windsor did resemble the new 12/6 Harley which was made by the Pressed Steel Company. The Windsor was listed at £268, with standard finish and equipment, £20 less than the Burnham which was the De Luxe model. It was a short-lived style, as for 1933 both it and the Burnham were replaced by the Berkeley.

Open Road Tourer – November 1926 to 1934

Introduced in 1926 as another version of the Clifton with which it ran side by side in production until 1930.

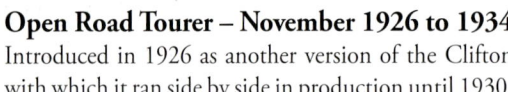

Below: Catalogue illustration of the 1930 New Open Road tourer.

There were quite a few differences from the Clifton in that there were separately adjustable front seats, the doors were wider and of an entirely different shape with T-shape handles, and the side curtains folded into the door linings. It was more expensive than the Clifton. The above illustration is from a 1930 model year sales brochure and is the Sixteen-Six version. The price of the Twelve-Four was £270. A revised body called the New Open Road was introduced for the 1930 model year with deeper doors, changes to hood and side screens, and a one-piece windscreen. This was at first offered only on the Sixteen-Six chassis, but for 1931 it became available on the Twelve-Four at £275 and then replaced the Clifton; the word "New" was soon dropped. The 1933 model had a slightly inclined windscreen and a belt moulding but no other differences. The Open Road lasted through the 1934 model year.

Salisbury Six-Light Fabric Saloon – 1930 to 1931

The new six-light fabric saloon replaced the earlier six-light fabric saloon in October 1930. The Salisbury was actually a Sixteen-Six; the same body on the Twelve-Four was called the Wycombe. Described as "a handsome saloon of Austin construction and remarkable for its silent running" it was priced at £335, but like the other fabric saloons introduced in 1930, it lasted in production for only about a year. Regrettably none are known to have survived.

Special Two-Four Seater – 1928 to 1930

In 1927 Austin had introduced the new style two-four seater without a name (see below) which was at first available in standard and "special" versions, the latter having a Triplex safety glass windscreen. A year later, Austin standardised Triplex glass in all windscreens, so from now on there was just the "Special" two-four-seater in the range, listing at £265 for 1929 although the price had gone up to £270 by March 1929. The car stayed in the catalogue through the 1930 season. Several examples are known to have survived.

Sportsman's Saloon – 1929 to 1930

The Sportsman was a two-door fabric-bodied sports saloon with generous accommodation for two in front and less generous in the rear, for "two or three additional passengers on occasion". It was designed to meet the needs of motorists who enjoyed touring, or participating in sporting events, and had "ample room for equipment", in part as it had a luggage locker at the rear, the first Austin saloon with this feature. As can be seen from the illustration below, the Sportsman

THE STANDARD AUSTIN BODY STYLES

A 1928 Open Road touring car. (Photo: David Cantor)

Far left: The same 1928 Open Road touring car. (Photo: Ian Brough)

Left: 1931 Open Road tourer. (Photo: Jim Dean)

Far left: The Salisbury Six-light fabric saloon in blue, an illustration from the 1931 model year catalogue.

Left: Catalogue illustration of the Special Two-four seater.

Two colour illustrations of a Special Two-four seater in New Delhi, India (Photo: Awini Ambuj Shanker)

Right: 1930 Special Two-four seater (Photo: Stephen Postlethwaite)

Far right: Catalogue illustration of the Sportsman.

1929 Sportsman Fabric saloon. (Photo: Bill Taylor)

Below: A fine example of the 1928 two-seater taken opposite Lickey Church, where Lord Austin is buried. (Photo: Philip Smallbone)

Catalogue illustration of the two-seater touring car.

was also available with the 15.9hp engine. Introduced in 1929, it was only in the catalogue for less than one season. The price for the Twelve-Four Sportsman in 1929 was £320, or £330 with a sliding sunroof. Very few were made, and at the time of writing, there was only one known survivor of this model.

Two-Four Seater – 1927 to 1928

After the two-four seater Hertford was discontinued, Austin realised that there was still a demand for a two-seater, so for the 1928 season, Longbridge reintroduced one without a name to be marketed simply as a two-four seater. By this time the Sixteen-Six was in production and the new two-four seater was of course available for this model, as well as for t he Twelve-Four. The body was redesigned compared to the Hertford, with a squarer box-like tail fully integrated with the main body, and side curtains which folded into the doors. It was said to combine all the advantages of an open touring car with the protection of a coupé. The price according to the 1928 brochure was £295, or £300 for a "special model" with a Triplex windscreen. After the first year, when Triplex glass was standardised, the model was listed as the "Special" two-four seater, see above.

Two-Seater – 1929 to 1930

Alongside the "special" two-four seater, in late 1929 Austin introduced a new body style simply called the two-seater. Instead of the bucket seats of the "special", it had a bench seat for two or even three people, but it still had a dickey seat. The tail had a new profile, rounded rather than square in side view, and the price was £255, less than the "special" two-four seater. For the 1931 season when Austin introduced more model names, this new two-seater became the Eton and the Harrow, see above.

Watford Four-Light Fabric Saloon – April 1930 to October 1931

Introduced in April 1930, this four-light fabric saloon was described as a smart and serviceable car for the man of moderate means. It was the first Austin body

THE STANDARD AUSTIN BODY STYLES

Left: The Watford fabric saloon in black, an illustration from the 1931 model year catalogue.

Right: Catalogue illustration of the Watford fabric saloon.

Left: Catalogue illustration of the 1934 Westminster saloon.

Right: 1934 Westminster saloon, owner and photo source unknown.

Right: Catalogue illustration of the Windsor saloon.

Below: 1924 Windsor saloon in striking Kingfisher Blue. (Photo: Peter Wright)

with a slightly inclined windscreen and rear-hinged front doors, adopted on all the following fabric saloon bodies. It differed from the Marlow model by having cloth upholstery and sliding door windows, and was correspondingly cheaper, as it sold for £275. It was available only in black with a cream line at the waist rail. The Watford had been discontinued by October 1931 so it was only in production for a year and a half, and at the time of writing there were no known survivors.

Westminster Saloon – October 1932 to 1935 on Twelve-Four chassis

The Westminster four-light saloon first made its appearance in September 1931 on the Sixteen-Six but the body became available on the Twelve-Four a year later, in October 1932. The design was based on the short-lived unsuccessful Austin Twenty Whitehall four-light model of 1931, with a luggage locker at the rear. The Westminster was modernised twice in 1934, at first with doors rather than louvres in the bonnet sides, and then with the cowled radiator. After the Twelve-Four had been discontinued in 1935, it carried on to 1936 on the Eighteen chassis.

Windsor Saloon – 1923 to 1929

The first Twelve-Four saloon was introduced in November 1923, and was given the name Windsor from the start. It was made until 1929 when it was superseded by the Burnham. There was however a short revival of the name with the introduction of the steel-bodied "New" Windsor in 1932, see above. The

Right: 1925 Windsor saloon looking very much at home in front of Mount Taranaki in New Zealand. (Photo: Peter Fry)

Below: 1925 Windsor Saloon. (Photo: Peter Fry)

Right: The Wycombe fabric saloon in brown, an illustration from the 1931 model year catalogue.

Below: Catalogue illustration of the York saloon.

Company produced 18,013 Windsor saloons (this figure in fact includes Burnham production for 1929).

Wycombe Six-Light Fabric Saloon – 1930 to 1931

According to the Austin brochure of late 1930, the Wycombe was described as the "Comfort Car", not only for it being comfortably equipped but because of its freedom from drumming due to the way it was constructed, which was exactly the same as any other Austin fabric saloon! – indeed the same body was offered on the Sixteen-Six chassis and was then called the Salisbury. Like the other fabric saloons of 1930, it had a slightly inclined windscreen, and all doors hinged at the rear. Production lasted one year from 1930 to 1931 and it was available at £299, with another £10 for a sliding sunroof. Regrettably, none are known to have survived.

York – late 1934 to 1935 on Twelve-Four chassis

The York was introduced in 1934, on the chassis with the long wheelbase of 10ft (3048mm), it had the new cowled radiator, and doors rather than louvres in the bonnet sides. It was intended to be fitted mostly with the 16 and 18hp six-cylinder engines, but the Twelve-Four engine remained in production for the taxicabs. It is known that 85 Yorks were supplied with the Twelve-Four engine and at least one still exists. It can be safely assumed that the Twelve-Four version of the York must have had one of the shortest production runs. The York when fitted with a division became the Chalfont (rather than the Iver), and both models could be supplied with occasional seats at extra charge. Supposedly the Chalfont body could be fitted to the Twelve-Four chassis but it is not certain whether any were made. By the time the 1936 brochures were printed, the 12.8hp four-cylinder engine had been discontinued but the York and Chalfont carried on through 1937, latterly just with the 18hp six-cylinder engine, and were then replaced by the new Windsor model.

1934 (December) York Saloon. (Photo: Peter Wright)

Summary of Longbridge body styles

Model name	Body type	From	To	Comments
Beaconsfield	Fabric saloon, four-light	Oct 1930	1931	Similar to Marlow and Watford but fitted with the 16/6 engine
Berkeley	Single landaulet	1923	1927	Designed to be chauffeur driven
Berkeley (BRT)	Saloon, six light, fixed head or saloon De Luxe	1932	1934	Body also used on the 16 and 18hp models
Burnham	Saloon	1928	1932	Introduced with the 16/6 model, it then replaced the Windsor on the Twelve-Four
Carlton (BRN)	Saloon, six-light	1933	1934	Body also used on the 16 and 18hp models
Chalfont (BTH)	Saloon, six-light, long wheelbase, with partition	Oct 1934	1935	Cowled radiator; similar to York; body mostly used on the 16 and 18hp models
Clifton	Tourer	1924	1930	Before 1924 simply known as Touring Car
Eton	Two-four seater	1930	1931	Similar to and replaced by Harrow
Fabric	Saloon, four-light	Oct 1928	1930	Replaced by Beaconsfield, Marlow, and Watford
Fabric	Saloon, six-light	Oct 1927	1930	Replaced by Salisbury and Wycombe
Harley	All weather coupé	1923	1925	Designed with doctors in mind, hence Harley (after the Street)
Harrow	Two-four seater	1931	1934	1931-32 fitted only with the 16/6 engine; from 1933 also with Twelve-Four engine
Hertford	Two-four seater	1922	1926	Hertford name introduced in 1924
Hertford (BRU)	Saloon, six-light, short wheelbase, fixed head or saloon De Luxe	Oct 1934	1935	Cowled radiator; body mostly used on the 16 and 18hp models
Iver	Saloon with partition	1927	1934	Initially based on the Windsor, then in turn on the Burnham, Berkeley and Carlton; the name was used for an 18hp in 1936-39
Marlow	Fabric saloon, four-light	Oct 1930	1931	Similar to Watford and Beaconsfield
"New" Windsor	Saloon, six-light	1931	1932	A cheaper model with all-steel body; replaced by the Berkeley
Open Road	Tourer	1926	1934	Similar to the later Clifton but with better hood and side screens
Salisbury	Fabric saloon, six-light	Oct 1930	1931	Similar to Wycombe but fitted with the 16/6 engine
Special	Two-four seater	1928	1930	Called just two-four seater in 1927-28
Sportsman	Two-door saloon	1927	1928	Also available with the 16/6 engine
Two-seater	Two-seater	1928	1930	Later named Eton and Harrow
Two-four seater	Two-four seater	1927	1928	In 1928 became the "special"
Watford	Fabric saloon, four-light	Apr 1930	1931	Similar to Marlow (and Beaconsfield), with simpler equipment
Westminster (BWN, BWQ)	Saloon, four-light, short wheelbase	Oct 1932	1935	Cowled radiator from late 1934; body also used on the 16 and 18hp models
Windsor	Saloon, six-light	1924	1929	Up to 1927 split windscreen, after 1927 one piece screen; the name was used for an 18hp in 1936-39
Wycombe	Fabric saloon, six-light	Oct 1930	1931	Similar to Salisbury
York (BRP)	Saloon, six-light, long wheelbase	Oct 1934	1935	Cowled radiator, a few with the 12.8 engine were made; body mostly used on the 16 and 18hp models

Note that Bob Wyatt (quoted in chapter 1) says that "The last car with the 12.8hp engine was built on 12 December 1936". When Bob said "car" presumably he meant "as opposed to taxi". This may be wrong, it is more likely that production of the Heavy Twelve-Four non-taxi stopped in the summer of 1935, and certainly the model did not feature in any Austin catalogue issued after January 1935.

Chapter Five

SPECIAL AND SPECIAL-BODIED CARS, AT HOME AND ABROAD

Whilst Austin provided a comprehensive range of body styles, all of which were designed to satisfy the needs of the majority of its customers, there were always some who preferred the coachwork for their new Austin to be slightly different from those which Longbridge could offer. For this, they were able to order their new car from one of the many alternative coachbuilders specialising in this type of work.

The coachbuilder would then order the chassis from Longbridge which would be sent complete in every respect except for the bodywork. Some styles offered by these companies would even be included in the official Austin brochures.

However, in order to safeguard Austin against the possibility of the coach builder going into liquidation, every chassis purchased had a small brass plate riveted to the nearside rear cross member of the chassis stating: *"PROPERTY OF THE AUSTIN MOTOR COMPANY LTD"*. That way, if the assets of the coach builder needed to be disposed of, at least the Austin chassis would be returned to Longbridge and no financial loss incurred. It is not known if this situation ever did arise. Coachbuilders which are known to have offered alternative body styles on Austin chassis are:

J Blake and Co Ltd	Liverpool
Chalmer & Hoyer (Hoyal)	Poole, Dorset, and Weybridge
Flewitt	Birmingham
Gordon & Co	Birmingham
Thomas Harrington	Brighton & Hove
Mann, Egerton & Co	Norwich
Martin Walter	Folkestone
Morgan	Leighton Buzzard
Mulliner	Birmingham
Startin	Birmingham
Tickford (Salmons & Sons)	Newport Pagnell

Blakes (J Blake and Co Ltd) was founded in 1871 with premises in Bold Street, Liverpool. Their work, at that time, was building private carriages, and coaches for the Post Office. They built Post Office vehicles for many years, while they also undertook coachwork on various motor car chassis including Austin. Blake later became a prominent Ford dealership but ceased trading in 1999.

1928 Hoyal two-seater coupé with dickey seat now resident in Germany. (Photo: Michael Eggenton)

SPECIAL AND SPECIAL-BODIED CARS

The chassis when sold alone includes :—
Dashboard.
Dashboard brackets.
Front flitch plates.
Top toe plate.
Bonnet.
Bonnet handles and fasteners.
Radiator cowl.
Radiator calometer.
Number plates.
Oil gauge.
Shock absorbers.

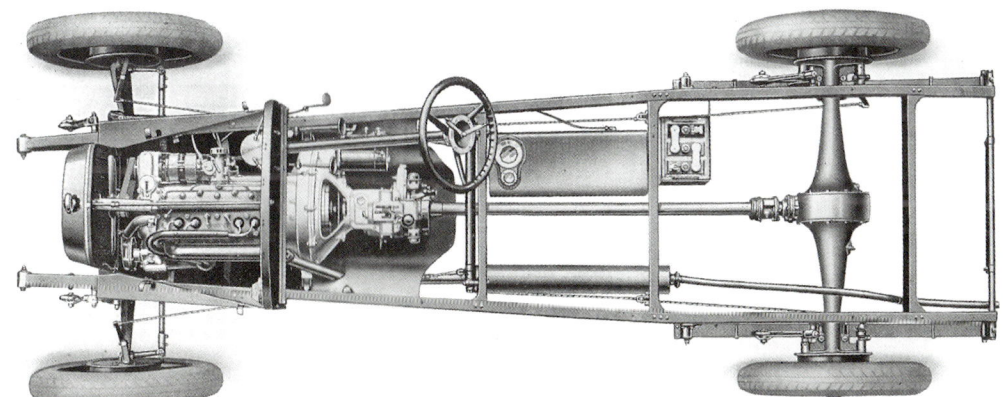

Equipment included, but not fitted :—
Spare wheel and tyre.
Spring gaiters.
Steering column support.
Five lamps and adapters.
Switchboard.
Cut-out.
Starter switch.
Dash lamp.
Speedometer.
Horn, bracket and switch.
Air strangler.
Magneto switch.
Starting handle.
Tool kit.

PRICE - £245 Complete at Works.

PAGE 17

Above: The chassis priced at £245 in the 1926 catalogue with four-wheel brakes but still 6-volt electrics.

Left: Page from Hoyal brochure. (Illustration courtesy of Suzanne Finch)

The AUSTIN TWELVE "HOYAL" Three-Seater Coupé

A 2-3 SEATER COUPE with an unusually wide, adjustable driving seat. The interior is panelled polished inlaid woodwork, and the coach-built head is covered with real leather, lined with cloth. This head folds down very neatly when not required. A comfortable double dickey seating two passengers brings the accommodation up to five.

Upholstered in leather or Bedford cord. Equipment includes clock, driving mirror, automatic windscreen wiper, electric horn, luggage carrier, and those accessories shown on chassis specification.

Coachwork by Messrs. The Hoyal Body Corporation Ltd., London, who take all responsibility for coachwork.

Price: £395
At London Depot.

PAGE 31

Above: The Hoyal Three-seater coupé as illustrated in the Austin Motor Company's catalogue (ref 561) published on 22 October 1926. (Illustration from author's collection)

Right: This 1924 Chalmer & Hoyer bodied Austin was built specially for The Rev. Churchill Julius, Bishop of Canterbury, New Zealand. (Photo: Barry Baine)

Chalmer & Hoyer (Hoyal) was founded in Poole, Dorset in 1921. In 1924 they opened a second factory in Weybridge. Between 1924 and 1928 they produced saloon coachwork for the Morris Oxford. They took out a licence to make fabric bodywork under the Weymann patents. In 1926 they became the Hoyal Motor Body Corporation. Their association with Austin was not prolific and they closed down in the August of 1931.

The 2/3-seater shown below was marketed under the name Hoyal, which was described in their catalogue as a three-quarter coupé. In the Austin Motor Company's sales brochure of October 1926 it is described as having an unusually wide, adjustable driving seat. The interior was of panelled inlaid woodwork, and the coachbuilt folding head was covered with real leather lined with cloth. Whilst described as a 2/3 seater the brochure states that the double dickey seat offers accommodation for two passengers, bringing the total up to five! The price in the Austin brochure was £395 whilst the price of the body alone was quoted in the Hoyal catalogue as £175.

SPECIAL AND SPECIAL-BODIED CARS

Above: Blue 2/3 seater Hoyal coupé. (Photo: T Clarke)

Below: The Flewitt advertisement dates from 1929 and features the Sportsman's close-coupled coupé at £337.10.0.

Flewitt was established in Alma Street, Birmingham in 1905. They built many bodies on Rolls-Royce chassis and at least one Weymann fabric body on a Bentley chassis. In the 1930s they came to specialise in custom bodywork on Austin chassis. Regrettably there are no known survivors of Austin Twelves with Flewitt coachwork.

Gordon & Co was established at Sparkbrook in Birmingham in 1921 initially to build bodies on imported American chassis such as Ford and Chevrolet, They began building bodies for Austin chassis in the mid-1920s. They gave their bodies names such as Pixie, Moth, and Elf for the smaller models, but also Royal, Regal and Imperial for larger cars with formal bodywork. Production ceased in 1939.

Harrington Thomas Harrington & Son Ltd was established in 1897 in Brighton, Sussex. Their work initially consisted of the building of horse-drawn vehicles such as landaus and wagonettes. As motor vehicles began to arrive Harrington was well equipped

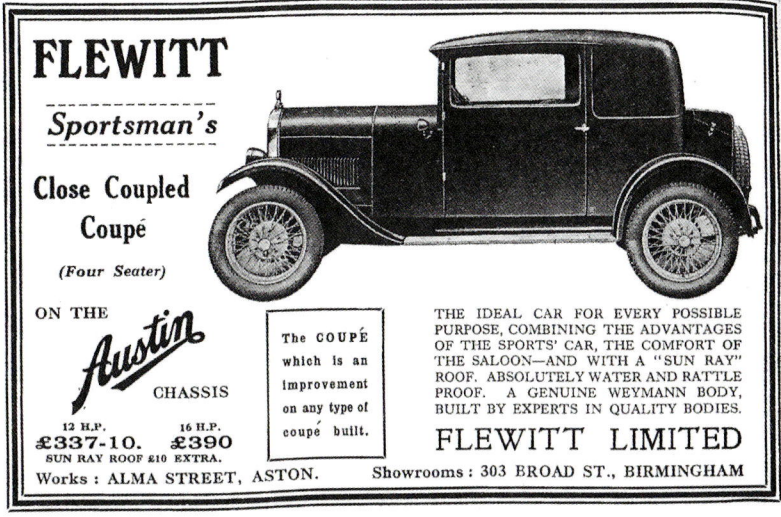

The 1926 Austin sales brochure featured the Gordon-bodied Twelve-Four Saloon Landaulet.

Below: The Austin shown in this advert from The Autocar *dated June 1929 is a Foursome Sun Coupé, also referred to as the Kay-Don model. Kaye Don (Kaye Ernest Donsky) was an Irish world record-breaking motor car and speedboat racer (1891-1981).*

Above: A blue Gordon bodied 1930 Austin Twelve-Four landaulet registration GC 5316. (Photo: D Dickinson)

to transfer their skills to accommodate this radical change.

By 1930, with a growing reputation for good quality work and a full order book the Company moved up the road to new and bigger premises in Hove. Whilst the majority of their work consisted of building buses and luxury coaches, they also entertained coach building on motor cars which included such names as Rolls Royce, Bentley, Bugatti and of course Austin.

SPECIAL AND SPECIAL-BODIED CARS

Left: The maker's plate attached to the dashboard of Mann Egerton coachbuilt bodies.

Right: Currently undergoing complete restoration, this is probably the only surviving example of a Mann Egerton two seater Austin coupé. (Photo: Paul Martyn, Bristol)

Left and far left: The two Harrington bodies shown are both of the fabric type built on the Weymann system. Both from around 1929, one is a four-light saloon, the other a two-door coupe with folding rear hood.

Left. KO 9012 is a two-four seater Doctor's Coupé by Martin Walter owned by Terry Wilson. (Photo by author)

Harringtons continued building coaches and special car bodies mainly for the Rootes Group up until 1966 when they ceased trading.

Mann Egerton & Co Ltd was founded in 1905 by Gerald Mann and Hubert Egerton. The works were based in Norwich and they had branches in several towns and cities in East Anglia, but they maintained an office and showroom in New Bond Street, London. They had a long association with Rolls-Royce. The company was bought out by its managers in 1986 and still operates as a car dealership.

Martin Walter Ltd was established in 1773 as a harness maker for horse-drawn vehicles which they also later began to manufacture. Based in Folkestone, Kent, they were pioneers of estate cars with their Utilecon bodies based on light vans and later became better known for the Dormobile camper van based on the Bedford CA, when, in 1954, they changed their name to Dormobile Co. They ceased trading in the mid-1980s and went into receivership in 1994.

Morgan Ltd. Morgan began in London back in 1762. In 1886 they moved to Leighton Buzzard, Bedfordshire, where they bought the business of WE King and the Battlesden Steam Carriage Works. The company began to make bodywork for Adler

Below: Bob Hughes's 1928 Morgan Fabric Saloon. (Photo: Bob Hughes)

59

Morgan's full page advert from The Autocar *dated 13 July 1928.*

motor cars in 1904, which were discontinued at the start of the First World War, since Adler cars were of German origin. When the war ended, Morgan began manufacturing bodywork for other motor car manufacturers, including Austin. According to official Austin records Morgan only manufactured two bodies for Austin chassis. They stopped exhibiting at the Motor Show after 1928.

Mulliner. Established by Herbert Hall Mulliner in Birmingham in 1887, this company specialised in the building of horse-drawn carriages. HH Mulliner and Herbert Austin collaborated on various projects while Austin was still with Wolseley in 1895-96. With the introduction of the motor car, and the subsequent decline in the demand for horse-drawn vehicles, Mulliner began to put their skills towards manufacturing motor car bodywork, and secured a large contract with Calthorpe. In 1917 Calthorpe took over the company and it lost its identity as a result. However, in 1924 Calthorpe went into receivership but the future of the coachbuilding side of the business was secured by a buy-out by the managing director who renamed it Mulliner Ltd. Mulliner prospered under its

The Mulliner four-door saloon as featured in the 1926 Austin catalogue

SPECIAL AND SPECIAL-BODIED CARS

new management and was able to secure a lucrative contract with The Austin Motor Company, specialising in producing Weymann style fabric coachwork for the Austin Seven. Based at Bordesley Green, Mulliner was taken over by Standard Triumph in the 1950s.

Startin. Thomas Startin set up his coachbuilding company at Aston in Birmingham back in 1840. The company was owned and run by the Startin family up until 1987 when it was renamed Startin Group of Companies. Startin later specialised in light commercial vehicle bodywork such as delivery vans, ambulances and hearses. The only known image showing an example of Startin coachwork may be found in the chapter on racing Austin Twelves. The car in question is currently undergoing a complete restoration.

Tickford (Salmons & Sons). Established in 1820,

Above left: 1923 Mulliner bodied two-seater tourer with dickey. Note the wooden spoked wheels. (Photo: M Rolls)

Above: 1925 Mulliner bodied Twelve-Four saloon. (Photo: Cairns Fulton)

Left: Mulliner two four seater from the Austin Catalogue of 1926.

Left: 1928 Mulliner two-four seater, original price £275. (Photo: Brab Hallows)

Right: 1927 Twelve-Four saloon by Mulliner. (Photo: Mike Gibson)

Above: 1928 Tickford All Weather saloon. (Photo: Peter Wright)

Right: 1933 Tickford Sunshine Cabriolet by Salmons & Sons. Although the car shown is a Sixteen-Six, the coachwork for the Twelve-Four was exactly the same. (Photo: Keith Laidlow)

Right: An advertisement which appeared in The Autocar for Salmons boasting of their Centenary, and showing two Austin Twelves fitted with coachwork which could be viewed on their stand at the Motor Show.

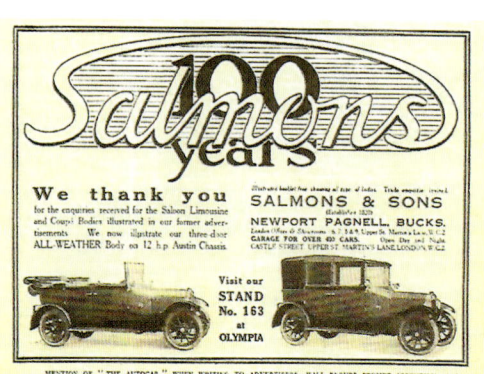

Salmons & Sons Ltd of Newport Pagnell, Buckinghamshire became famous in the inter-war period for roll-top sunshine saloons and later drophead coupés, where the folding action of the roof was operated by a winding handle. These were marketed under the name Tickford which was subsequently adopted for the company. In the post-war period, the company was taken over by Aston Martin Lagonda, and for many years the Tickford works was the main Aston Martin factory.

The Sizaire-Berwick – an Austin by another name

In chapter 1, Bob Wyatt mentioned the Sizaire-Berwick and said that he could not understand why, after the Austin Motor Company had itself come out of receivership, Herbert Austin decided to invest money in another company that was in a parlous financial position.

The British company was set up jointly by the French Sizaire brothers, Maurice and Georges, with the London motor trader and importer of French cars, Frederick William Berwick, in 1913. They were financed by Scottish marmalade heir and archaeologist Alexander Keiller. Chassis were originally built in France but were mostly fitted with bodywork and sold in England. The company became renowned for producing luxurious motor cars that were every bit as good as those manufactured by Rolls-Royce.

In fact it did not go unnoticed by Rolls-Royce that the Sizaire-Berwick's radiator design bore a remarkable resemblance to their own, which resulted in Rolls-Royce taking them to court. However, when it came to examine the facts, it was found that while Sizaire-Berwick had actually registered their design for the radiator, Rolls Royce had omitted to do so. Then in 1914 came the war and the matter was consigned to the back burner until it was over when, after a sum of money had been handed over, the matter was amicably resolved, with the outcome being that Sizaire-Berwick

Above: Advert for Sizaire-Berwick 23-46hp, circa 1923, but the 13/26 is also mentioned, costing £590. (Photo: Vintage Austin Register Archives)

Left: An advertisement for Tickford (Salmons & Sons) which appeared in the October 1929 edition of The Austin Magazine. *The body for the Twelve-Four was listed at £170. (Author's collection)*

agreed to change their radiator by making it slightly V-shaped and by placing a thin aluminium strip from top to bottom down the centre of it.

In 1915 Sizaire-Berwick had built a large factory at Park Royal in London for making aeroplanes. They planned to increase production of a new car with a 4.5-litre four-cylinder engine based on the 1914 model. However, during the early years after the war, like many other motor car manufacturers they found it difficult to regain their place in the market. Try as they may, production never got back to how it was prior to 1914, and to make matters worse, Georges Sizaire and Frederick Berwick both decided to leave the company, and nor long after so did Georges' brother Maurice.

A receiver was appointed in 1920, after they had produced just 200 cars. In 1922 Herbert Austin was approached to see if he could help the company in any way. The Austin Motor Company had only just come out of receivership, saved from annihilation by the introduction of the Twelve-Four and of course a few months later, the Austin Seven.

Austin, together with Dubliner Harvey Du Cros

Sizaire-Berwick 13-26hp tourer (Photo: Vintage Austin Register Archives)

Sizaire-Berwick 13-26hp, with smartly attired chauffeur (Photo: Vintage Austin Register Archives)

The 1926 Twelve-Four Holden-bodied open touring car owned by Anthony Mealing shows a distinctive raked windscreen, which Herbert Austin would not have approved of! (Photo: Anthony Mealing)

Junior, came prepared to help in any way they could, providing they could profit by their actions. Du Cros had helped to start up the Austin Motor Company in 1905, and was involved with many other companies both in the UK and in France. Perhaps Herbert Austin saw this as a way in which his company could increase the sales of the Twelve and Twenty models, and, if things did not work out well at Longbridge, he would have acquired a foothold in another car manufacturing company, which he would be well placed to buy into.

Herbert Austin and Harvey Du Cros agreed to join the board of directors, and The Austin Motor Company agreed to supply Sizaire-Berwick with the Twelve and Twenty horsepower chassis, which would then be fitted with their own distinctive design of radiator and coachwork.

By October 1922, Sizaire-Berwick launched a new range of cars to the buying public. The 12hp Austin based cars were marketed as the 13-26 which cost £450 and the 20hp as the 23-46 at £590. In addition there was also the 26-52 which was described as "An entirely new chassis designed by Herbert Austin". This turned out to have a six-cylinder engine of 3397cc, rated at 25.3 RAC hp, and was fitted with a three-speed gearbox. Whilst certainly bearing all the hallmarks of an Austin design, it had no counterpart in Austin's then-current range of cars. The first six-cylinder Austin Twenty was not to appear until 1927, with the Sixteen-Six becoming available later that same year.

At the 1923 Olympia Motor Show, Sizaire-Berwick had just three examples on display but not the 26-52 which had by now been removed from the range. During the early part of that year only a few 26-52 cars, fitted with standard touring coachwork, were sold at a price of £1225. It should be noted that a Bentley cost the same amount, and a Vauxhall 30/98 £5 less.

By the following year the whole range of cars had been discontinued and plans were put in place to replace them with just one single model for 1925, a 15hp actually rated at 13.9hp and to be sold between £695 and £835 depending on the body style. It is not recorded how many of these 15hp cars were actually sold and there had never been any road tests reported in the motoring press. Later that year the British Sizaire-Berwick story ended. Small-scale production of the large 4.5-litre four-cylinder car continued in France for a few more years.

Fredrick Berwick, after leaving the company, became involved in the manufacture of the Windsor and the British Salmson motor cars, and died in 1960. Maurice Sizaire, after leaving in 1922, went on to establish the short-lived Sizaire-Frères car company in France. He died at the age of 91 in 1969. Georges died just two years after leaving the company in 1924.

Colonial coachbuilders: Australia and New Zealand

Because of high duties imposed on imported vehicles in Australia and New Zealand around the time of the First World War, a motor car imported complete with bodywork would be considerably more expensive than those with bodywork made locally. These duties were intended to protect the local bodybuilding industry. Motor manufacturers such as Austin found a way around this by just sending completed chassis, which would then have similar styles of coachwork to those available in Britain, but built by local coachbuilders.

With regard to vehicles imported into Australia, since 1914 two thirds of imports had to have locally made bodywork. In New Zealand the coachbuilders petitioned the Government to impose an import duty, which they did in 1915. Due to the war the New Zealand duty lapsed, but was re-instated in 1926, finally to be abolished in 1934.

During the 1920s there were at least 12 coachbuilders in New Zealand and 36 registered in

the Sands & McDougal trade directory in Australia. Only those listed below are known to have built bodies onto Austin chassis, by virtue of examples which exist today.

Australia

Holden. JA Holden established an upholstery and saddlery business in Adelaide in 1856 which also made other leather equipment for the carriage trade. They built their first motor car body in 1914 on a Lancia chassis. In 1919 the company changed its name to Holden's Motor Body Builders, and tended to concentrate on coachwork mainly for American imports. By 1924 Holden became the exclusive bodywork supplier to General Motors of America. By 1929 they were employing 3400 staff and turned out 40,000 bodies. They were bought by General Motors in 1931 and the name was changed to General Motors-Holden, but for some years afterwards, Holden continued to supply bodywork to other manufacturers. In 1949, Holden introduced the first specially-designed all-Australian built Holden cars which for many years dominated the Australian market. The company continued into the 21st century building cars mostly based on Opel designs, but the last car was made in Australia on 20 October 2017. The Holden name was then used for imported cars until discontinued in 2021.

Cheetham & Borwick was founded in Melbourne by Yorkshireman, John Cheetham at the end of the First World War, he was joined by Jack Borwick who had immigrated to Australia from the Orkney Islands in Scotland. They mainly built coachwork on Rolls-Royce, Delage, Mercedes-Benz, Armstrong Siddeley and Austin chassis, but also built many bus bodies. John Cheetham died in 1955 and left the business to his son, who specialises in building custom-built cars, and restoring veteran and vintage vehicle.

Melbourne Body Works. Melbourne Motor Bodies was established in 1907 by Alexander Smith after he had been involved with companies which built cars back in the late 1890s. In 1909 they moved premises to Carlton and became associated with the Ford Motor Company. By 1923 they moved yet again, and re-named the company Melbourne Motor Body & Assembly. They bodied almost anything, from Amilcars to Rolls-Royces, and of course Austins. They are also known to have built ambulances. After having changed their name to Ruskin Motors they were eventually bought out by The Austin Motor Company in 1950.

Colonial Motor Engineering & Coachwork Company. According to the owner of the Austin Tourer featured below, the coachwork was manufactured

An early photo of Cheetham & Borwick's premises located at 47-49 Cardigan Street, Carlton, with bus bodies in evidence.

Above left: John Blythe's 1929 Roadster with Holden coachwork. Note the unusual bonnet louvres. (Photo: John Blythe)

Though not a Twelve-Four, this 1929 Sixteen-Six with coachwork by Cheetham & Borwick provides an example of this company's work. This, too, has angled bonnet louvres. (Photo: David Clayton)

1928 open touring car with coachwork by the Melbourne Body Works. Note the slightly angled windscreen. The car is now in the UK. (Photo: Robert Husband)

A late 1928 Austin open touring car with coachwork by the Colonial Motor Engineering and Coachwork Co. of Brisbane. (Photo: B Lowdell)

This 1927 Austin catalogue was issued by the main Austin Distributors Pty Ltd, based in Bourne Street, Melbourne. It announces the new Exclusive "Empire" model with the long-stroke engine which replaced the original short-stroke engine in 1926; the car shown may have the wider track of 4ft 8in. (Photo: Tony Johns from the David Zeunert collection)

by the above company which was based in Brisbane, Queensland. Regrettably no further information can be found regarding this particular company.

New Zealand

CL Nielsen & Co were coachbuilders located in Dannevirke, Hastings, and specialised in providing bodywork on imported Oakland and Hudson chassis, but were not known as being major players in building bodies for Austins. The Twelve-Four saloon illustrated

Right: The main New Zealand dealership Magnus Motors exhibiting the Austin Twelve-Four at the Wellington Motor Show in 1923. The two-four seater is on the left behind the 20hp chassis located next to the five-seater touring car. (Photo: The New Zealand Vintage Austin Register archive)

below is thought to be the only surviving example of Nielsen's work, and even that replaced the open tourer coachwork which was fitted to this car when it was imported from the UK in 1925. The saloon coachwork however closely resembles that of the Windsor saloon, but is slightly narrower. One unusual feature of the Nielsen coachwork was the vertical-opening windscreen which provided the driver with a free flow of air whilst driving. The original car number was 3TT 7447, and the second T confirms that it was an open tourer.

The Zealandia. The Zealandia was the trade name for bicycles made by Oates, Lowry & Co of Christchurch. In 1905 they became a car dealership, and established branches in Wellington, Napier, Ashburton and Timaru. In 1929 and 1930, the Zealandia name was used for a four-door, four-light fabric-bodied saloon built on an Austin Twelve-Four chassis. The construction of the Zealandia coachwork was similar to the Longbridge made fabric saloons which were very popular around that time. Where they differed from other Twelve-Four coachwork was that the backs of the front seats were designed to fold back, making them "ideal" for camping.

The Zealandias were marketed through Austin Agents Magnus Motors and JG Ingram & Co Ltd. Through his research on this model, Denis Le Cren has discovered that according to an advert in the *Nelson Evening Mail*, JG Ingram had three Zealandias in stock

SPECIAL AND SPECIAL-BODIED CARS

Two views of the only-known Nielsen-bodied Austin Twelve. (Photos courtesy of Peter Fry)

This photo of the seats converted into beds was published in The Austin Magazine *for July 1929 so the design must have attracted some interest at Longbridge.*

The text in this advert reads as follows:
Now the world-famed Austin Twelve chassis is offered with a distinctive colonial-built 4-door closed fabric body at the economical price of £395. The result of this combination of superlative coachwork and mechanical excellence is a car that is outstandingly different. The Austin "12" is neither a light nor a heavy vehicle, yet it has the advantage of each. The economy and reliability of this British-built quality car is known wherever motor highways exist. With the backs of the front seats folded back the Austin "12" Zealandia saloon makes an ideal camping car. This particular Austin model, whilst being a perfect town car, is ideal for camping and weekend runs. Come and examine this popular British-built quality car in our showroom. Its better value will immediately be apparent.
(Advertisement courtesy of Denis Le Cren)

but none were ever sold and they were subsequently returned to Magnus Motors.

The first known example was offered for sale on 19 December 1929 at a price of £355. *Chassis no. 59314, car no. 5TS 943A, engine no. 5991L.*

The second was offered in grey on 6 June 1930 at £345. This too was returned unsold, to Ingram's Blenheim branch. *Chassis no. 60432, car no. 5TS 1097A, engine no. 60504L.*

The third, also priced at £345 was returned, unsold, to the Magnus Motors Wanganui dealership on 13 June 1930. *Chassis No. 60466, car No. 5TS 1102A, engine number 60764L.*

It is not known why the Zealandia did not attract the intended sales, but it may be worth noting that an imported Twelve-Four Burnham saloon could be purchased for just £380. Regrettably no Zealandias have survived. Other New Zealand Coachbuilder known to have built bodies on Austin chassis include Seabrook-Foulds of Auckland (who were also Austin importers), and David Crozier of Christchurch.

Chapter Six

AND THEY WERE RACED TOO!

The Twelve-Four ready for the New Zealand Light Car Cup in 1924. (Photo: the New Zealand Vintage Austin Register Archive)

When the Austin Twelve-Four was first made available to the motoring public, it was described simply as a light touring car – ideal for the family man who wished to drive and maintain the car himself. No mention was made about racing it, although the larger Austin Twenty had of course shown itself to be quite a fast motor car in its own right when raced against other, more powerful cars at race tracks such as Brooklands. It soon became obvious that the lighter Twelve-Four was not going to be left behind.

It wasn't long before owners of these "light touring motor cars" decided that the Austin Twelve could be coaxed into going considerably faster than the Austin Motor Company claimed they could, and we commence this chapter with an extract from *Flat to the Board,* an account of an event written by Douglas Wood and AR Messenger on how in New Zealand the Twelve-Four was pitted against other cars more suited to racing.

The annual Muriwai race meetings organised by the Auckland Automobile Association (AAA) of New Zealand, were held along a stretch of the beach at low tide. The course took drivers straight down the beach for 4 miles, where they did a U-turn at a marker and then raced back to the start. The race consisted of 6 laps making the total distance covered 50 miles.

The meeting for 1924 was held on March 22nd, when the organisers introduced a new event called the New Zealand Light Car Cup. This allowed cars of up to 3 litre capacity to enter, though in later years, this was reduced to 1.5 litres. On this occasion the event attracted approximately 850 spectator cars, which were driven onto the beach, and over 5000 spectators arrived in charabancs and on foot, Once on the beach they were able to wander all over the course causing considerable problems with crowd control and disruption to the races.

Dexter Motors Ltd, the Auckland Austin Agents, had entered a new Twelve-Four with two-wheel brakes

and 760x90 (probably 765x105mm) beaded-edge tyres. The car was actually owned by a Mrs MA Mill, and was driven by her son Douglas.

Before the race commenced the body, wings and running boards were removed to be replaced by a much lighter, more streamlined affair constructed from plywood. The engine received nothing more than a good tune-up. The driver's seating was lowered to reduce drag, and he could therefore only just see over the bonnet. Other than these modifications the car was considered to be "just as it left the factory" a fact which saw the slogan "Stock Model" emblazoned on the car for all to see.

There were six starters lined up across the beach, and the crowd by now had become well behaved and kept well away from the course. The flag dropped at 2.30pm, and all got away to an even start. It was not long before Douglas in the Austin was in the lead, having started in second gear, thus avoiding one lengthy gear change. Armitage driving the FIAT was going well, although dropping behind the Austin to such a degree that by the end of the first lap the Austin was 200 yards ahead, a gap which was widening.

At the end of the second lap the position was much the same with the Austin, getting covered in sand and water thrown into the air from its wheels, yet increasing its lead, Armitage was well behind in the FIAT now secure in second place. Way behind was

Breadnell driving a Buick-Four followed by Bedford in an Essex, which eventually pulled out. The Austin continued to increase its lead, eventually crossing the line a clear winner. The FIAT came second with almost half a mile between it and the Austin.

Douglas Mill's time for the 50-mile race was an impressive 46 minutes, achieving an average speed of 65 miles per hour. Considering the fact that the seven turns at each end of the course had to be negotiated at very slow speed due to the proximity of the crowd, which was especially worse at the start end of the course, the Austin's maximum speed must have been closer to 70mph.

Mill, as the winner, was accorded a great reception as he drove up to be decorated with the champion's flag by Mr Jas A Warnock. In addition to the flag he also received the New Zealand Light Car Cup and miniature, and a gold Omega wrist watch.

Following the race, the car was returned to Dexter Motors' garage, the original body, wings and running boards were refitted and the car returned to the care of Mrs Mill, apparently none the worse for the experience.

Meanwhile back in the UK at an event held at Brooklands in August 1925, an Austin Twelve, entered by Sammy Holbrook, the Austin Motor Company's Sales Manager, and driven by Austin Seven racing driver, R Cutler, managed to lap at 72.7mph (117 km/h). The car, it should be mentioned was fitted with a four-seater aluminium body, from which the hood, mudguards and running boards had been removed. The bonnet had been painted black, the rear seats were covered in a fabric material, and as well as the Boyce Motor-Meter mounted on the radiator cap it also had an AA badge displayed for good measure. The wheels were fitted with Dunlop herringbone tread tyres. The speed recorded in an earlier race was 74.33mph (119.6 km/h).

A couple of months later Morgan & Co. of Leighton Buzzard launched what was described as a "Sports Austin" which had a two-seater body, flared wings of an unusual shape, a pointed tail and no running boards, and on the same day as that was announced in *The Autocar*, *The Motor* informed readers of a "hotted-up" Austin Twelve Sports Saloon manufactured by The Allan-Bennett Company which was capable of 60mph (97 km/h) available at a price of £575.

Confirmation of its high speed reliability was claimed after a non-stop run at Brooklands when the car covered 102 miles (164km) in 108 minutes, "a fine achievement". Balancing of engine components was part of Austin's manufacturing process so although various methods were claimed as to how the engine was modified, it was the compression, which had been raised considerably, that increased the power. A charge

Another image of the racing Twelve-Four. (Photo: the New Zealand Vintage Austin Register Archive)

This is a full page advertisement which appeared on 31 July 1924, in which the Company heralds the fact that an Austin Twelve-Four had achieved second place in a hill climb held at Shelsley Walsh. The driver, it should be noted, was Louis (Lou) Kings, the Company's test and competition driver. (Photo from The Auto Motor Journal)

This advert suggested that by replacing the car's original cylinder head with the LAP ohv head, for just £30, owners could obtain better acceleration and more power when ascending hills. The AF Lago mentioned is Anthony Lago who was also the British importer of Isotta-Fraschini and was involved with the Wilson pre-selector gearbox. He later took over and ran the French Talbot car company.

John Raine's Startin-bodied two-seater with race number 161 at Silverstone in 1962. (Photo: Vintage Austin Register Archive)

of £25 was made if you wanted your engine "hotted-up" with a claimed increase of 10bhp and a speed of 10mph! By 1928 the firm of Allan & Bennett was sold, and Cyril Bennett became an agent for selling Austin cars.

By 1929 the LAP Engineering Company had developed an overhead-valve cylinder head for the Austin Twelve-Four engine. *The Autocar* reported on the LAP conversion as "A Test of Overhead Valves: Experiences with a 12hp Austin touring car fitted with LAP head." It was used for some time as a staff car having covered 3000 miles with a fair degree of success. The LAP head was combined with the "hotting up" process of the Allen-Bennett Motor Company, but with no indication that this contributed anything to the conversion. The tendency of the side valve engine for pre-ignition was not a problem for the OHV head, which gave much improved all-round performance and maintained a top speed of over 60mph. It would have cost around £40 to have the OHV head fitted and so it would appear that the addition of an OHV cylinder head, replacing the one supplied with the car, was an assured way of gaining a few extra mph.

We now move on to 1962, when two owners of Austin Twelve-Fours, Norman Cox and John Raine, decided to enter their cars in the VSCC's (Vintage Sports-Car Club) annual Inter-Register event which was held at Silverstone. Norman's Austin was a 1926 Clifton registration number YN 5063, and was his everyday mode of transport. John's Austin was a 1925 Startin bodied two-seater, registration number TT 4379. Norman's Austin had suffered from clutch slip, which was still giving cause for concern almost up to the start of the race.

However the two Austineers booked in at Race Control and set off to do a ten-lap practice run. John sped off with Norman following. Norman was pleased to find that he could reach 55mph and experienced no further problems with the clutch.

Both cars began to show a good turn of speed. Norman recalls that taking the corners in the Twelve was well within the car's capability, but in doing so it tended to lose speed which then had to be regained. It was well past Beckets that Norman was able to build up to the Austin's maximum speed of 60mph again, then into Woodcote holding full throttle without braking but coming out at 45mph, into Copse at 52 and holding full throttle, without any appreciable loss of speed. 60mph round Maggots, sharply braking, but coming out at less than 40 and then a slow build-up of speed again to 60-plus on the straight into Woodcote. Norman's fastest lap was just over 48mph, whilst John's was just over 50.

The actual race was over five laps of the circuit, and although Norman remembers very little of the actual race, he does recall being overtaken at least twice by every car which left the start after him, but did actually recall overtaking the four cars which had started before him. Norman could not recall how he was placed, but John came third with a time of 10 minutes, 36.4 seconds. The

The three Austins seen in this photograph from 1963 are Norman Cox's Clifton tourer, number 171, which was sporting a newly fitted hood, Peter Heath in his Clifton and Ray Danaher in his two-seater sports. (Photo: the Vintage Austin Register Archive)

event was won by a Humber at 9 minutes 47 seconds and second was a Fiat at 10 minutes 12.2 seconds.

A year later in April 1963, the annual VSCC Inter Register event again saw entries from owners of the Austin Twelve. On this occasion no fewer than five Austins, three Twelves and two Sevens were entered, which constituted a full team. However on the day of this event the weather was typical of April, with heavy showers making driving conditions somewhat hazardous.

The practice race went quite well until Ray Danaher, whilst travelling at speed, came into contact with a press hoarding causing some slight damage to the car. However a Frazer Nash which also came into contact with the same hoarding a few minutes later did not come out of it too well and was badly damaged. At 14.30 the cars lined up with two others on the starting grid. The three Austins were placed together along with a Fiat 501 and a G.N. The race comprising of five laps was without incident and was won by a Sunbeam. Ray Danaher came in a creditable fifth behind two Fiats and an Alvis. Norman Cox came in seventh and Peter Heath tenth.

The Austin shown on the following page, known affectionately as "The Green Thing" started life (as such) in 1996-97 and was made up from what the owner describes as a load of scrap! The 1929 chassis originally supported a Clifton open tourer body, but this had been removed many years previously when it was converted to a truck for use on the farm from where it was now rescued.

In order to fulfil its role as a farm truck, the chassis had been hacked about quite a bit, and needed some repair work doing to it before any other work could commence. When the remains were discovered, the engine was still in place and in a reasonable condition but it was stripped down for overhaul and modifying which saw the camshaft and followers re-profiled, and the flywheel was considerably lightened. It was fitted with a Ricardo head and larger valves, and also twin carburettors. The exhaust manifold was replaced with a four-branch one and the whole engine was properly

"The Green Thing", a Twelve-Four modified for speed and hill climbing. (Photo: Norman Tidd)

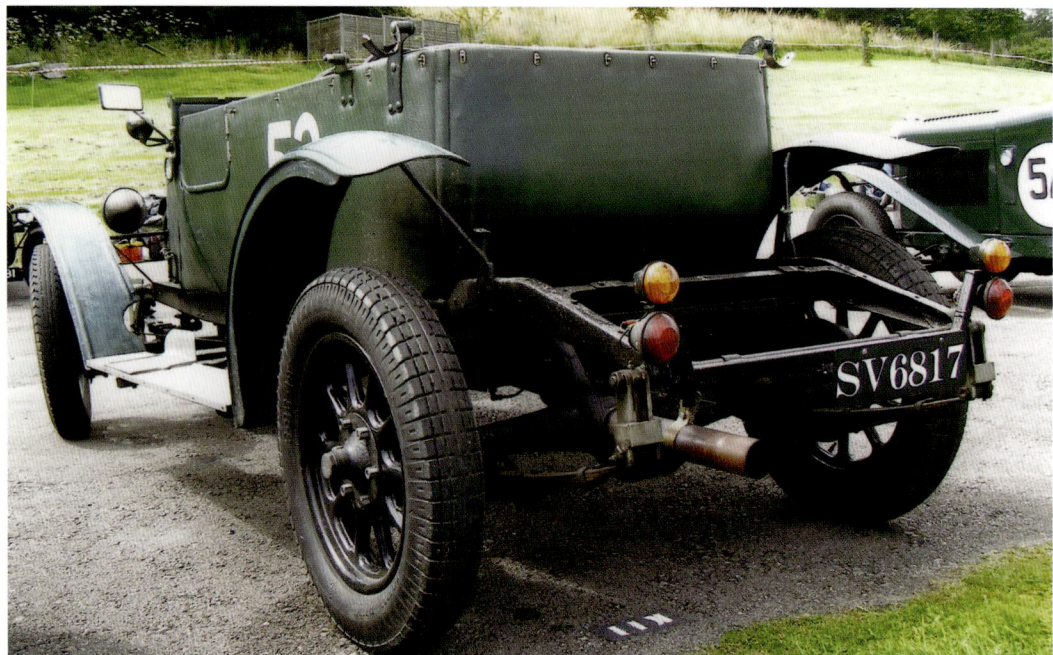

A rear three-quarter view of "The Green Thing", with its Bentley body. (Photo: Norman Tidd)

balanced. It is understood that the body was originally fitted to an early Bentley, whilst the wings had started life on a Model T Ford.

The car was completed by the year 2000, and began to compete in VSCC events with modest success. In 2003 it was entered for its first hill-climb at Harewood House, which proved to be very successful. Where speed was concerned "The Green Thing" could achieve 60mph in third gear and even more in top, and could hold its own against the more "sporty" cars such as the Alvis 12/50s, 2-litre Lagondas, and was even found to be quicker than the 3-litre Bentleys! In all, the modified Austin Twelve-Four received eight VSCC awards during the time it was raced. "The Green Thing" has since appeared in several television programmes which included *Peaky Blinders*.

The Austin Twelve-Four, in spite of it being regarded simply as an owner-driver family car, has over the years proved to be quite a competitive vehicle in its own right, on the understanding that it requires a few tweaks here and there from those who want to prove that to be the case.

Chapter Seven

BROCHURES, ADVERTISING AND PUBLICITY

The first sales brochure

With the launch of the Austin Twelve-Four came a very impressive sales brochure (reference no. 252) which was issued on 1 January 1922. It featured just three models which were shown together with prices, "complete at works". None of the three different body styles were as yet given names. These were to be added a few years later.

It was stated that "The Austin Twelve embodies all the essential features of a high grade car. The chassis has been so proportioned that various types of coachwork can be satisfactorily accommodated." The brochure then went on to describe the various coachwork styles.

The first model to be shown was the two-four seater, which was described as a car with smart appearance, graceful in outline and contour, and of a well-balanced design. It had ample seating with the driver's seat being adjustable to provide the best position for the easiest and most efficient control. It also had a two-person dickey seat which folded away in the neatest manner possible.

With regard to weather protection, it was mentioned that it had a double-deflecting screen and a smart hood which was easily raised. In the worst weather, full protection against its effects was ensured by the fitting of detachable side curtains, which were part of the standard equipment. The car was offered in Dark Blue and Grey, with all the fittings being nickel plated of the highest quality. The price for the two-four seater was £550. By 1924 it was to be known as the Hertford.

The next model to be illustrated was described as a four-seater touring car, which was later to be known as the Clifton. This model was described as being an ideal family car offering an excellent amount of accommodation, thus enabling parties to tour in comfort, whilst the appearance of the car was exceedingly graceful and stylish.

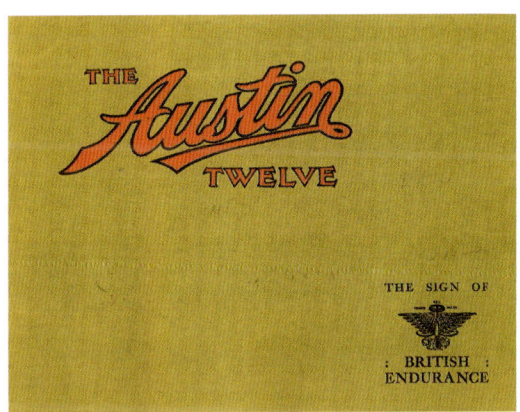

On the brochure cover, the Austin logo was claimed to be "the sign of British Endurance".

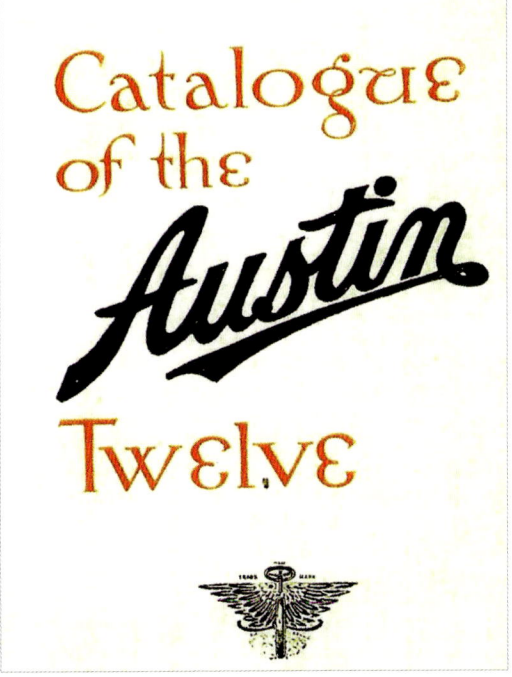

Title page of the brochure.

The two-four seater shown with hood raised.

Below: The Austin Twelve two-four seater car, a sturdy vehicle completely equipped.

The tourer shown with hood raised.

The coupé with the hood lowered.

The four-seater Austin Twelve, an excellent family car at a moderate price.

It then went on to describe the manner of front seat adjustment, and the provision of a hood and side screens which made it thoroughly weatherproof in the most unpleasant of weather. A tool box was located immediately behind the front seat, which also doubled as a foot rest for the rear passengers. The standard colours were again Blue or Grey, but alternatives were available, should the purchaser wish for something different. The seating was of course in real leather. The price for the four seat touring car was £550.

The final model shown was the four-seater all-weather coupé, which was designed to satisfy the demand for a light totally enclosed car, with a very high standard of elegance. When it was desired to use the car as an open one, the hood could be folded back very neatly, and the framework of the windows dropped out of sight. When the hood was raised, the occupants of the car were protected in a most effective fashion against discomfort from the elements.

As with the previous two models, the brochure went on to describe the means of front seat adjustment, and also pointed out that the length of the pedals could be adjusted to suit the driver. It was a two-door car, and the brochure praised the fact that it had a door either side of the front seat (at the time, many cars only had a door on the passenger side of the front seat, as the gear lever and hand brake were often mounted on the right), which were of such width that entry into it was very easy, and then explained that access to the back seats was gained by moving the front seats forward. Upholstery was again in real leather of a colour to harmonise with the selected colour of the car, which would have been either Blue or Grey. The price of the four-seater coupé was £675, but with a leather hood, and painted to choice, it cost £695. It was later to be called the Harley.

The chassis was noted as being "substainally constructed of the finest materials, completely equipped, economical in use, and built to last."

The power unit was of the "single" type (more commonly called unit construction), combining engine, clutch, and gearbox, and was suspended at three points, a method protecting the unit from stresses. By adopting aluminium pistons and light moving parts, high engine speeds were obtained without vibration, thus giving rapid acceleration, sweet running, and great flexibility. All the transmission gears and road wheels ran on ball bearings.

The necessary adjustments to such components as steering and brake gear were readily accessible; the

BROCHURES, ADVERTISING AND PUBLICITY

The Austin Twelve Coupé, a high grade car suitable alike for long journeys and social engagements.

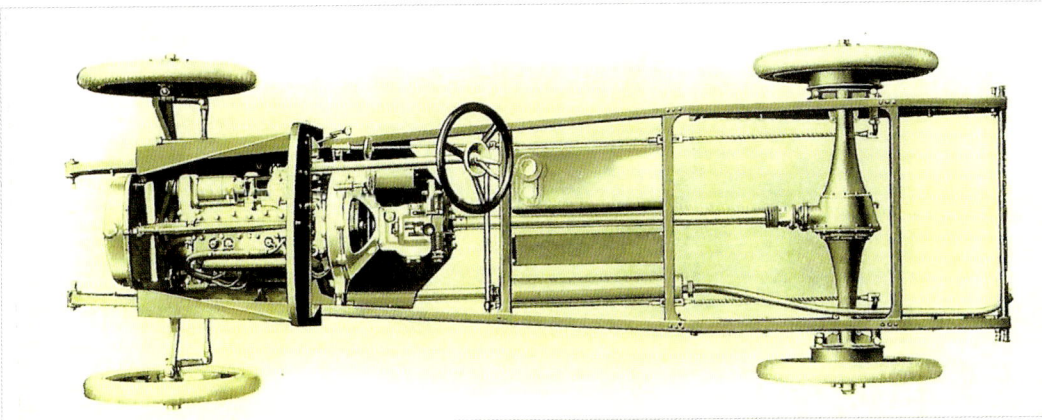

The plan view of the chassis shows the controls, and the position of the petrol tank under the driver's seat, with the battery box alongside on the other side of the prop shaft.

Side view of chassis showing position of controls

pedals could be altered to suit individual requirements. The usual ignition and throttle control levers were situated above the steering wheel. Electric lighting and starting equipment was complete in every way, and consisted of a two-unit 6-volt set. Switch gear, speedometer, and other instruments were neatly arranged on a flush type board. A complete set of tool equipment was supplied with the car.

Adverts which sold the Austin Twelve-Four

In the following section we take a look at just a few of the hundreds of advertisements which appeared in the

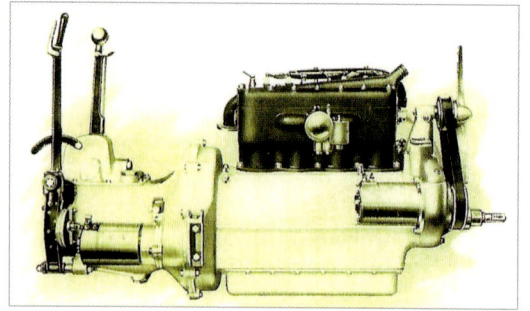
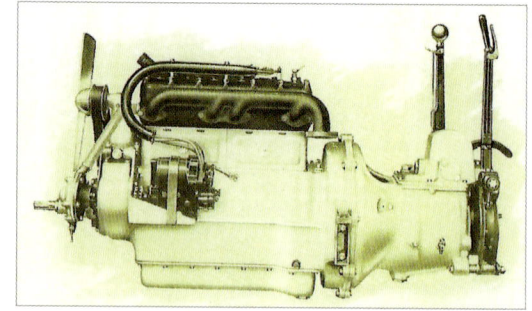

Right: Off-side (right-hand side) view of power unit, showing the Zenith carburettor bolted on to the cylinder block, the starter motor behind the flywheel, and dynamo at the front of the engine, with belt drive to the fan.

Far right above: Near-side (left-hand side) view of engine, with the magneto mounted at the front, and also the exhaust manifold. In both views we see the short gear lever and its gate, as well as the transmisison brake and the hand brake with its quadrant.

Right: This must be one of the earliest adverts for the Twelve-Four taken from The Auto Motor Journal *dated 27 April 1922. A neat pen and ink illustration of the Twelve ascending a hill with an almost full load shows would-be customers what it looked like, describes what to expect from this new car and of course mentions its price. The hefty initial price of £550 was to be considerably reduced over the lifetime of the Twelve, as further adverts will testify.*

BROCHURES, ADVERTISING AND PUBLICITY

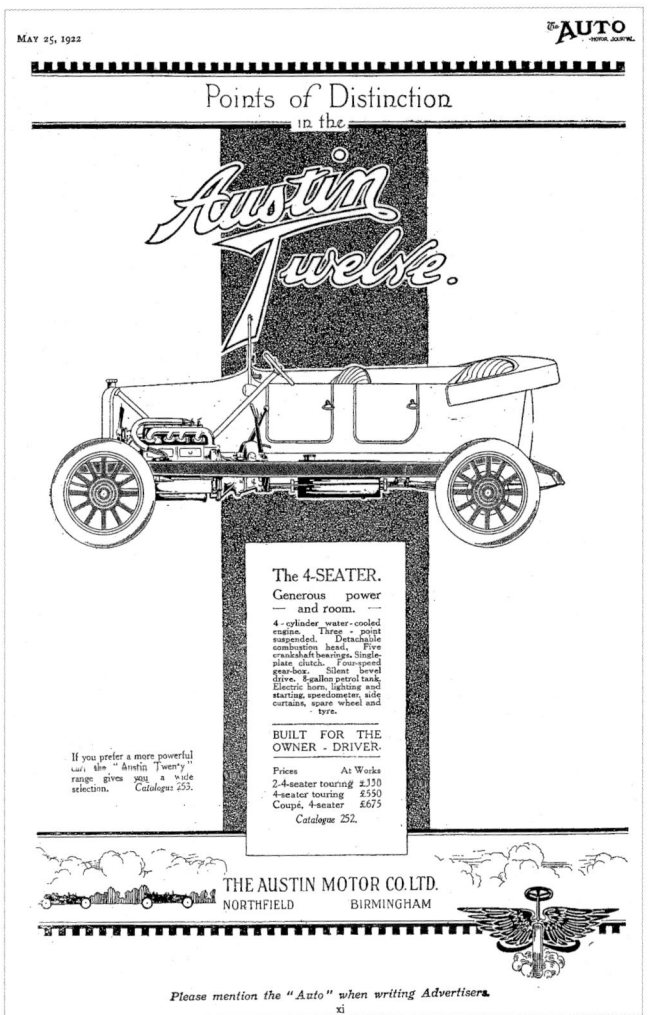

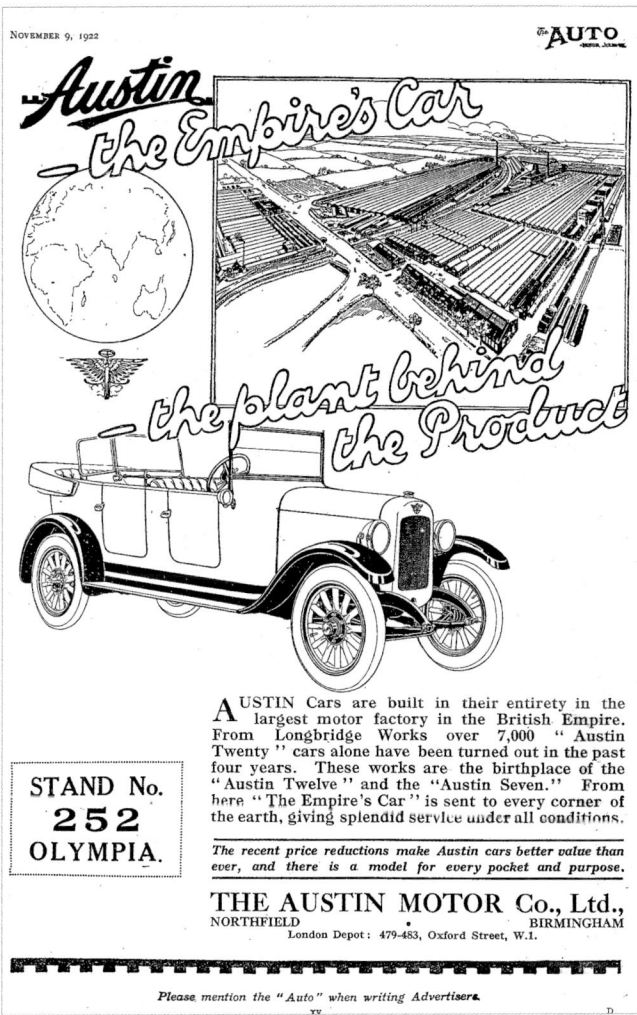

Still using line drawings to illustrate the adverts, the next one, also from The Auto (Motor Journal) *is dated 25 May 1922. The blurb commences "Generous power and room", and then goes on to tell the reader that the Austin Twelve has a "Four cylinder water cooled engine, Three-point suspended, Detachable combustion head, Five crankshaft bearings, Single plate clutch, Four Speed gear-box. Silent bevel drive, 8-gallon petrol tank. Electric horn, lighting and starting, speedometer, side curtains, spare wheel and tyre." – All for £550! This advert was one of a series of three, each depicting one of the models which were available: the two-four seater touring car, the coupé four-seater and the four-seater touring car shown here, later to be known as the Clifton.*

The next advert, published just a few months later on 9 November, once again promotes the four-seater open tourer. It appeared at a time when the annual Motor Show was being held at Olympia, so the Company was keen to point out to visitors that it could be seen (and no doubt ordered) from stand number 252. The Company had been denied a stand at the previous year's Motor Show due to the fact that it was in receivership. Now out of receivership, the Company was keen to advise potential customers that the Twelves were "built in their entirety in the largest motor factory in the British Empire. From Longbridge Works over 7,000 Austin Twenty cars alone hahave been turned out in the past four years." In very small print, the advert also advises that the price had recently been reduced.

press during the life of the Austin Twelve from 1922 to 1934. It is noteworthy that most of these adverts were featured in quality periodicals such as *Punch* and *Country Life*, in addition to the popular motoring press such as *The Autocar, The Auto Motor Journal*, and *The Motor,* and that many of them took prime positions in such publications, often taking up the entire page.

As we progress through the years we cannot help but notice the way in which the adverts are designed to catch the eye, and in some cases the seasons are used to emphasise the ability of Austin cars to cope with whatever the weather conditions may throw at them at that particular time.

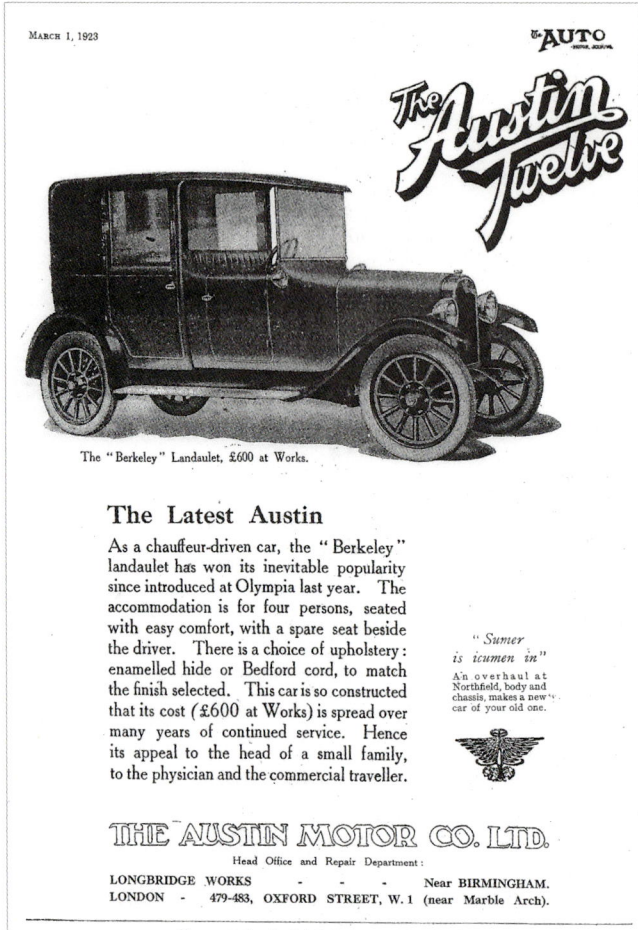

Above: The next advert framed in an Austin radiator comes from the Austin Advocate *magazine published shortly before the London Motor Show. (3-11 November 1922), and, like the previous advert draws attention to the fact that the prices had been "substantially reduced". The Austin Twelve-Four models are featured to the right of the advert.*

Above: By 1923 a new Austin Twelve was available, and was the first to be given a name, the Berkeley landaulet. The Berkeley was designed as a chauffeur-driven motor car, and had been displayed for the first time at the previous year's Motor Show. It had accommodation for four persons, with a spare seat located beside the driver, and looked very similar to the taxicabs which were to appear several years later. The purchaser was given a choice of upholstery in either enamelled hide or Bedford cord. The Berkeley was designed to appeal to "the head of a small family, the physician and the commercial traveller", all for the sum of £600. An interesting note appears above the "Wings & Wheel" logo where Austin offered the facility of "An overhaul at Northfield [i.e. Longbridge works], body and chassis, makes a new car of your old one" – but was that offer ever taken up?

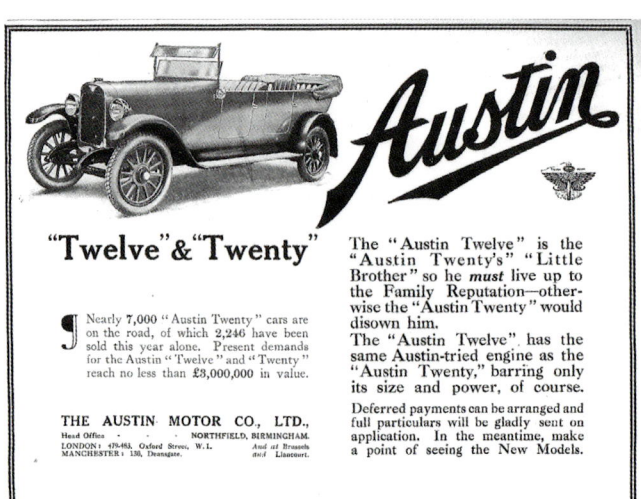

Left: In order to advise potential customers that the Austin Motor Company was now financially buoyant again following a spell in receivership, this advert from an unknown source is keen to advise them that (as in the previous advert) nearly 7000 Austin Twenty cars were on the road, of which 2246 were sold in the year the advert was published, adding £3,000,000 to the Company's finances. The model illustrated is once again the Twelve four-seater open touring car.

BROCHURES, ADVERTISING AND PUBLICITY

Below: "Buy an Austin and banish care" was the catchy slogan used to promote the products in July 1923, and again it was the four-seater touring car which was featured. The advert was keen to express the virtues of owning an Austin with the text: "Full assurance of constant, willing service is felt with Austin cars, and the ready response of their powerful engines makes driving a delight. In an Austin one buys years of motoring free from care". It is worth noting that the price, as stated in a previous advert, had now been reduced by £100 to £450. The slogan "Buy an Austin and banish care" was used by the Company for several years.

By 1924, The Austin Twelve-Four appeared with a saloon body, known as the Windsor. Promoted as being "ideal as a luxury car of medium capacity", the Windsor design "meets present-day demands to a nicety". Features included large pockets on the backs of the front seats, an interior driving mirror, a windscreen wiper, lever window lifters and locks to all doors. The price? £550.

Right: This full page advertisement by Morrison Motors of Melbourne, in The Australian Motorist *magazine of 7 July 1924, describes the Twelve as the 12/28 model (the 28 being the claimed brake horsepower). It was available for £515 with a twelve month guarantee. Austin cars were held in very high regard in Australia as Herbert Austin spent several years learning his trade there, and even had an Australian wife. On one such advert (from Larke, Hoskins & Co. Ltd of Sydney), the writer described Austin thus: "A Master Product! Genius – a big word, but not so big as to convey adequate expression of the Master Mind behind the Austin Cars. In every Austin is reflected a lifetime of study, culminating in the triumph of a work well and truly done". In 1926 Wilfred Anderson with his wife Ellen and dog Kerry completed a tour of Australia in their Twelve-Four tourer. Kerry was bitten by a snake and was buried by the roadside. (See An Austin Anthology I).*

By now the Windsor saloon at £455 was becoming very popular and a highly respected addition to the Twelve range, and as the advert was keen to point out, it was indeed a beautifully finished car, which provided ample accommodation for five persons. Now, with the Company promoting its cars with the slogan "Austin means Excellence", the Windsor was indeed a very well appointed and well-built motor car.

By 1924, and as first seen at the Motor Show of that year, the 25 September edition of The Auto Motor Journal *ran an advert under the heading "SAFETY FIRST", which advises potential purchasers that the "Austin cars now have four-wheel brakes" which are "Simplicity itself: no universal joints to wear and rattle; absolutely weatherproof." To further reassure those who were not totally convinced that four wheel brakes were a good thing, it then went on to say that tests had stretched over twelve months and the car's steering was totally unaffected. Adjustment to all four brakes was carried out by simply turning one handle. From a safety point of view, the application of the brakes ensured the ability to stop at once without skidding, and full braking power was always available whilst maintaining a high average speed.*

The advert from The Auto Motor Journal *of 17 July 1924 clearly shows the Clifton tourer, but still not named as such. However by now the Company described it as a five-seater car, whereas before it was marketed simply as having a seating capacity for four. The reference to Special models having a clock, luggage carrier, spring gaiters and a rear screen would indicate that there were two levels of trim available for this model. The Standard model was listed as having canvas tyres, wood instead of steel wheels, less luxurious equipment and painted only in plain grey.*

One of the first Austin Twelves to appear was the Harley, though, when first launched in 1922 it was simply referred to as the Austin Twelve four-seater coupé. Set against a winter scene this advert promotes the benefits of owning a Harley as being a car for all-the-year-round comfort and of unfailing readiness for hard work.

By 1928, Austin had started to produce the Fabric Saloon, a short-lived trend which, whilst looking very smart when new, was easily damaged, and proved difficult to repair. The appeal of the fabric body was that it was lighter than the metal body and eliminated drumming. Their popularity lasted until about 1931.

In this Country Life advert of 1929 there is an image of Sir Herbert Austin, who was promoting the Clifton Tourer. In Austin's own words, he explains the origins of the Twelve: "When the Clifton Tourer was designed I had built into it strength and stamina to withstand the constant stress and strain of hard daily service. That meant sound construction and the best of materials. These qualities, which give to the Clifton amazing reliability and economy in running, have made this model an outstanding favourite with motorists – not only in this country but in almost every part of the world. In this car I have given you all you want in speed, power and comfort and at a price of £245 it is unquestionably the finest Touring Car value obtainable today. Very roomy for five persons, the Clifton is generously equipped, and by virtue of its quality will always command the highest re-sale price." Well, with regard to the last sentence H.A. was certainly correct there

"AUSTIN – The Car That Sells Itself!" An inspiring advert which appeared in The Motor Trader of 20 November 1929, was not in itself an accurate statement, because had that been true then this very advert would not have been necessary. However the text certainly gives the impression that Austin motor cars are a good investment, "economical to buy and run, hardworking, and command ready resale". Since the advert was aimed at the trade, it is stressed that "trade terms are so remarkably generous that every Austin sold is a gratifying piece of business."

By 1932 Austin had launched their new range of cars which included the 10/4, the 12/6 and the Light 12/4, intended to replace the original Twelve-Four which now began to be referred to as the Heavy Twelve-Four in order to differentiate between the two. However with the success of the taxicab, which was based around the rugged reliability of the 12.8hp engine, Austin found that it just could not be replaced, and this was also endorsed by popular demand from its customers who still required their new Austin be powered by the 12.8hp engine, and so both the 11.9 and the 12.8 engines were manufactured side by side up until 1935. In fact the 12.8hp engine continued to be produced up to 1940 – simply to satisfy the demand from the Taxi trade and, by that time, the Ministry of War.

It is interesting to note how the prices of the Twelve-Four changed over the years, altering almost on a monthly basis, designed no doubt to attract customers by offering a good quality product at an affordable price; a table will be found in the appendix.

Cigarette cards and postage stamps

Motor cars have often been considered as a suitable subject for featuring on postage stamps, and before that, cigarette cards, which were collected by children in the 1920s and 1930s at a time when just about everybody smoked! Such cards actually go back to the 1880s. Their format was dictated by the shape and size of the cigarette pack, but they would also slip easily into a schoolboy's blazer pocket and were no doubt eagerly studied and swapped during break time. There were series of many different subjects issued by various cigarette makers, and motor cars were a perennial favourite, together with for instance cricketers and football players; these subjects had the advantage that new series could be issued at regular intervals without repeating exactly the same motor car or sportsman. Below follow just a few examples where the Austin Twelve-Four was included in cigarette card series.

This advert for the Austin range appeared in Punch *magazine of 12 September 1934. This advert is keen to promote the "Beauty of Line" of the new body styles of the 1934-35 models, which had been designed by Ricardo Burzi and featured the cowled radiator. This left little or no room for the now outdated Heavy Twelve-Four, but, in the right hand column of the advert are prices for the various models which were available and yes, here is a mention of the Heavy Twelve-Four which reads thus: "The Twelve (12.8h.p., 4-cyl). Westminster Saloon £325, Carlton Saloon £305, Iver, with division £315, Berkeley Saloon £295 and the Berkeley Fixed Head Saloon £275." The names appear to refer to the 1934 models with the chrome-plated radiator. This was the final advert in which the 12.8hp Austin Twelve-Four was mentioned. It was never referred to again in any future advertisements, and soon ceased to be manufactured.*

The first card, from the series "Motor Car Bonnets" came from Illingworth Cigarettes and was one of 25 cards which showed just the front end of what appears to be an Austin open touring car with its hood erected. The small vent in the scuttle would indicate it to be around 1925.

BROCHURES, ADVERTISING AND PUBLICITY

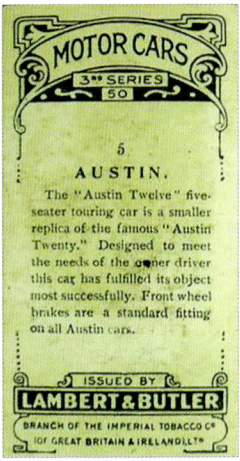

The second card was Number 5 in a series of 50 cards issued in the mid-1920s by Lambert & Butler. From the reverse side of the card we can determine that according to the company, "The 'Austin Twelve' five seater touring car is a smaller replica of the famous 'Austin Twenty.' Designed to meet the needs of the owner driver this car has fulfilled is object most successfully. Front wheel brakes are a standard fitting on all Austin cars." The fact that it mentions front wheel brakes but not the name Clifton would indicate the card was issued in 1924.

The next card is a bit of a mystery, in that it only shows the front of what could be either a Twelve or a Twenty. There is no further information as to who produced it or exactly what the Austin model really is.

The next card, issued by the United Tobacco Company in the mid-1920s, gives very little away in its title other than it is an Austin. On the reverse of the card the car is described as a limousine which can seat seven people, so we can deduce that it is in all probability a Twenty.

Postage stamps

Most postage stamps featuring motor cars have probably been issued in modern times and are aimed at collectors, rather than being intended to stick on letters. In Britain, probably the first stamp with motor cars was issued in 1966 in a series about technology: it featured the Jaguar E-type and the BMC Mini. One of the most featured cars on postage stamps must surely be the Austin Seven, including the 1982 Royal Mail series of British cars where it was doubled up with an Austin Metro. In 2010, the late Brian Norfolk published a book which included many examples of this popular little Austin on postage stamps. However, shown below are just a couple of examples of the Austin Twelve, which have also been featured on stamps.

The final cigarette card is from a set "Motor Cars" issued by WD & HO Wills in the late 1920s and depicts the various processes employed at Longbridge during the manufacturing of the Austin Twelve-Four. These are doctored photographs from Austin factory originals and the two lines of completed chassis seen here are actually of the Sixteen Six; some of the original photos can be seen in chapter 3 of this book. The "Austin Six" script, which can be clearly seen on the radiator cores in the original photograph, has been removed from the illustration featured on this card. In fact the card does not appear to mention the name Austin at all.

The first postage stamp issued in 2011 is a 5 Rupee example from Sri Lanka which depicts a 1928 Twelve-Four Clifton tourer. The car still exists in Sri Lanka and is understood to be running very well.

The next Austin to be depicted is contained within a set of nine stamps issued in 2000 by the Kyrgyzstan Postal Service, all of which are British-made motor vehicles of the vintage or post vintage period. The Austin portrayed is a 1930 truck, with registration number OG 1892, which is owned by Mathew Gresalfi of Virginia Beach, USA. It would appear that the truck originally started life as an open tourer, and was re-registered in 1986.

The next postage stamp is of a 1926 Austin Twelve-Four Two-Four Seater Special, which is featured on a 10 Rupee stamp issued by India Post in 2017 to commemorate the means of transport in India through the ages. The car is owned by Awini Shanker of Delhi, who took several years to restore it. Many of the original parts were missing and replaced by those which have come from other vehicles, such as the Marchal head lamps which were originally fitted to a Bugatti that was scrapped in the early 1950s. The very same car is featured in chapter 4 of this book.

Finally, the two images shown above were produced by the Post Office as part of a service called "Smilers". This enabled members of the public to have their own images put onto first class postage stamps. The stamps illustrated feature the 1925 Windsor Saloon owned by Derek Bryant. The service was discontinued in 2018.

Chapter Eight

THE TWELVE AS A WORKHORSE: THE TAXI STORY IN PEACE AND WAR

How the Austin Taxi came about

Herbert Austin had toyed with producing an Austin-based taxicab as far back as 1906, but he considered that there was little future in pursuing their production and decided to concentrate all his efforts on manufacturing high-quality private cars. However that was to change when a young man from London managed to persuade him otherwise.

The "young man" was William Overton. After having successfully fitted several taxicab bodies to Austin Twelve-Four chassis for use in Manchester, he could see the potential for Austin taxicabs which could be deployed elsewhere in the UK, but specifically in London with its very strict regulations. The Manchester taxi bodies were manufactured by The Elkington Carriage Company, a Chelsea-based firm of coachbuilders.

William's company, Mann & Overton, was based in London and had for many years been a main supplier of cabs for the capital, but they also had a branch in Manchester where the Twelve-Four cabs were trialled. The reports on how successful they were and liked by those who drove them, were all that William needed for him to take the train up to Longbridge to speak to the man himself, in an attempt to persuade him to modify the chassis in order that they could conform to the requirements of the Metropolitan Police's Public Carriage Office, the authority which was responsible for regulating the construction and use of Hackney Carriages for use in and around London.

At first Herbert Austin refused to see this fellow from London, and expected him to return by the next available train, but William's dogged determination caused him to remain outside Herbert Austin's office until he was eventually told that Austin would be prepared to listen to what he had to say.

The outcome, as we now know, was that Austin did agree to modify the Twelve-Four chassis to comply with the required turning circle of 25 feet (circa 7.5 metres), and thus being able to provide the capital with the finest fleet of purpose-built taxicabs the world would ever see. As well as the steering being modified, and a more upright column installed, the taxi was fitted with rod-operated rather than cable-operated brakes on the front axle.

The first (officially) modified Twelve-Four was fitted with a taxicab body by the coachbuilders Dyer & Holden, and was sold to a Mr AW Barker, who was highly respected in the cab trade. He paid £380 (cash) for it, and it was licensed on 7 June 1930. A further 271 Austin taxicabs were to be purchased during that year with over 400 in 1931.

Finally, a true story relating to the Austin taxicab came from Arthur Waite, who was Herbert Austin's son-in-law. Herbert Austin and Arthur had travelled from Paddington Station by taxi to their office in London's Oxford Street, where Arthur got out, and his father-in-law continued on to the RAC in Pall Mall. Normally they would have been chauffeur driven, but on that particular day the chauffeur was otherwise engaged taking Irene, Arthur's wife, out shopping.

On reaching the RAC Austin disembarked

Mr Barker's 12/4 taxicab parked outside the main office block of the Longbridge works. (Photo: The London Vintage Taxi Association)

from the cab and advised the cabby that his shock absorbers needed adjusting, before rushing up the steps and leaving the doorman to pay the fare from the Company's account. The cabby then said to the doorman "What does the old b....r know about shock absorbers?" to which the doorman replied, "He should know, he made your cab!"

Another true tale also from Arthur Waite was when Austin was being driven down London's Regent Street, he was overtaken on the inside by a taxicab. When the chauffeur drew alongside the cab, Austin lowered the window and advised the cabby of his poor driving, then ended by saying "Well at least you are driving an Austin taxicab!"

1934 Birch Brothers bodied taxicab in the Southwold Museum. (Photo by author)

The taxicab body styles

Longbridge certainly had the means by which coachwork for a London-style taxicab could be produced in large quantities but The Austin Motor Company chose not to undertake such work, instead the completed chassis were sent to various coachbuilders, mainly in the London area to be completed. Presumably these companies had ample experience with taxi bodywork and had worked with Mann & Overton.

Birch Brothers. A London-based company which started back in 1837, operating and building horse-drawn cabs, and later horse-drawn buses. In addition to running a fleet of buses and taxicabs, the company also manufactured the coachwork. Birch Bros built a small number of Austin taxicabs mainly for their own use, and one which is known to have survived is currently on display in the Southwold Museum in New Zealand.

Cape. The Cape taxicabs were a bit of an oddity in that they were manufactured by more than one company to a design submitted in 1929 by a Mr W Gowan, who originated from Cape Town in South Africa. They were originally intended for the Morris-Commercial G1 chassis, and over 100 were to be built between 1930 and 1937.

The Cape cab was unusual in that instead of the conventional two hinged passenger rear side doors, it had two sliding doors mounted in curved tracks across the vehicle behind the driver's seat and luggage platform. This allowed entry and exit without the

THE TWELVE AS A WORKHORSE

Another Birch bros-bodied taxicab also in a museum. (Photo source unknown)

danger of doors swinging open over the road or the pavement, although it would seem difficult to arrange for extra occasional seats to be fitted. Some of them had a proper driver's door. The Cape design was taken up by several of the well-known coachbuilders including Strachan, The New Avon Body Co, and Arthur Mulliner of Northampton.

A Cape cab body on an Austin chassis. (Photo: the London Vintage Taxi Association)

Christopher Dodson. This company specialised primarily in the building of buses and commercial vehicles. It had been established at the turn of the century with their factory and head office in Cobbold Road, Willesden, London NW10.

Dyer & Holton. Established just after the end of the First World War, Dyer & Holton were based at 4-6 Crownstone Road, Brixton and also had a workshop in Camberwell. The coachwork for the taxicab illustrated on the next page was one of 196 manufactured in 1923 for The London General Cab Company by Dyer & Holton to be mounted on Citroën chassis. When the Citroën cabs were due to be scrapped, the bodies were considered to be far too good to be broken up and were removed from their chassis and placed into storage.

A decision was then taken to re-mount the bodies onto Austin Twelve-Four chassis, which met with the approval of the Public Carriage Office, and they then continued in service for a further 30 years. This strange mixture of chassis and bodywork led to them being referred to as the "Chinese Cabs" due to them being "a bit of a (Chinese) puzzle". Dyer & Holton ceased trading in 1936.

As it appears today after having been in storage for a number of years, the 1933 Austin taxicab with coachwork transferred from a 1923 Citroën cab.

Elkington Carriage Company. Compared with many of the other coachbuilders, Elkington was a relative new comer to the business, having only come into existence just after the First World War. Elkington, unlike many of the others, did not have the experience gained through the building of horse-drawn carriages.

Three further views of the fully-restored "Chinese cab", including one which shows the delightful interior, possibly trimmed to a higher standard than when it was new! (Photos courtesy of Keith Laidlow)

One of the original Citroën taxis fitted with this style of body. (Photo: the London Vintage Taxi Association)

THE TWELVE AS A WORKHORSE

1937 Low Loader taxicab with coachwork by Goode & Cooper. (Photo: Nicholas Dann)

Based in Chelsea, the company was believed to have been started by Messrs Taneborne and Kendall of whom little, if anything is actually known. However it is understood that Taneborne left the company in 1922. By 1928 they had re-located in Chiswick, West London where, in 1931, the company started building bodies for Frazer Nash. As mentioned above, they built the bodies for William Overton's Manchester taxis.

Their first attempts to break into the London Taxi business were frustrated because their bodies did not conform to the Public Carriage Office specification, as they favoured a V-shaped windscreen over the officially approved flat screens. However, those built with the V-screen were accepted in the provinces, and versions with flat screens were built specifically for London. Regrettably no examples of this company's taxicabs are known to have survived.

Goode and Cooper. Established in 1840, and based in Brixton, South London. The company made their name initially by building horse-drawn carriages. It is also known that they were instrumental in operating their own fleets of taxicabs, and built bodies for the British-built Unics which were known as KF1s. Goode & Cooper became involved in the manufacture of coachwork for Austins in the early 1930s and continued to do so until the outbreak of the War.

Unlike cab bodies manufactured by other coachbuilders, they fitted the hood irons inside the hood, offering an immediate recognition point. Before the Second World War, almost all taxicab bodies were of the landaulet type body with a folding hood over the rear seat, but this type of body was banned after 1945.

The same cab photographed several years earlier outside the King's School, Canterbury where Vernon Austin, Lord Austin's son, was tutored. (Photo from author's collection)

1933 High Loader with Goode & Cooper coachbuilt body. (Photos courtesy of Robert Seabourne)

1934 Jones bodied taxicab parked outside the former Jones Bros Factory in Westbourne Park. (Photo: Warren Rushton)

Just a year younger, the 1935 "Fishtail" Jones bodied Twelve-Four taxicab. (Photo: Brian Bromwich)

Right: Two 1938 "Flash Lots", a name given by cabbies because they were considered to be rather "flashy"! These bodies were mostly made by Jones. (Photo source unknown)

THE TWELVE AS A WORKHORSE

The Jones bodied cab which was £5 more expensive than those from other coachbuilders. Interestingly, the registration number on the Jones cab shows that the photo was of a 1936 model.

Jones Bros (Coachbuilders) Ltd. Established in 1861, the company was based in Lonsdale Road, Westbourne Park, London W11. By 1935 they employed a workforce of around 150 craftsmen engaged in manufacturing bodies for Austin taxicabs. On average the company was capable of turning out between 100 and 150 cabs per year.

Three features by which a Jones-bodied cab may be recognised are the curly front end to the roof luggage rack and the rear body panel being tucked

The interior of the Jones Bros factory showing probably the last of the taxicabs in the process of being manufactured in 1939, now with the cowled radiator which had been used on the cars since 1934. (Photo: the London Vintage Taxi Association)

A 1937 Ricketts bodied taxicab, registered DGW 271. (Photos courtesy of "Hitch-a-lift" Wedding Hire.)

The open door to the spare wheel compartment of another Ricketts cab CYH 948, also showing the typically tiny rear window in the hood. (Photo from author's collection)

under. On later models, this rear panel was flared out giving rise to the name "Fish Tail" and the spare wheel was stowed away behind a boot lid. A Dunlopillo filling was always used for the passenger seating. The Jones cab was considered slightly more superior to those produced by other coach builders, and in consequence cost £5 more.

J & H Ricketts. James & Henry Ricketts (Coachbuilders) were first recorded in the Business Directory of London dated 1884 with premises both in Coburg Street and Drummond Street, Euston, North West London. By 1909 they were describing themselves as "Coachbuilders & Cab Proprietors" – which meant that they owned taxicabs which they rented out to licensed drivers on a daily basis. The Ricketts cabs of the 1930s were notable for having the spare wheel enclosed within a small boot at the rear, and that the seats were upholstered in leathercloth (Rexine) instead of leather. Just five Ricketts cabs are known to have survived.

The Strachan-bodied taxicab, with some fancy beading on the rear quarter panel to split the two-tone colour scheme.

Strachan (pronounced "Strawn"). The origins of this company go back to 1894 when Walter Brown started a small coachbuilding business in West London's Shepherds Bush. A year later he was joined by a Mr Hughes, and the partnership of Hughes and Brown was established. By 1900 with the coming of the motor car, they were quick to change over to building the bodywork for this new mode of transport, and in fact claimed to be the first to do so.

In 1907 James Strachan (formerly manager of Adams-Hewitt, Taxi Cab Operator), joined the partnership and the name of the company was changed to Brown, Hughes & Strachan. They then moved the business from Shepherds Bush to new premises a few miles up the road at North Acton. In 1911 the company even built their own motor cars, known as the Aberdonia, the range included a landau called the Park Royal which resembled a horse drawn landau – but production ceased in 1915.

In 1914, just before the start of the First World War Walter Brown and James Strachan resigned from the company and started up their own business which they established in Kensington, to be known as Strachan & Brown. During the War they built ambulances and many other military related vehicles. By 1921 they had moved into new premises also in North Acton where they specialised in building bus, charabanc and later, coach bodies.

In 1928 Walter Brown severed his connection with James Strachan and joined Duple, the coach builders, as a director. The following year, at the age of 64, James Strachan died from a brain tumour. The company now registered as Strachans (Acton) Ltd, then changed it again to Strachan's Successors Ltd following a period of financial difficulties.

Strachan's association with Austin came in 1930 when they were contracted to build bodies for Austin Taxi chassis. During the Second World War they once again turned their production facilities over to military vehicles. After the war Strachans became part of the Gilspur Group, and in 1963 moved their entire operation from Acton down to Hamble in Hampshire, finally ceasing business in 1974.

It is worth noting that the company also produced "knock-down" taxi kits for the London General Cab Company, who then assembled them onto Austin Low-

1938 Strachan Low Loader when owned by the author. (Photo from author's collection)

1937 Strachan-bodied Low Loader cab. (Photo: C Hutton)

The Strachan factory at North Acton showing a line of completed and licenced taxicabs. (Photo: The London Vintage Taxi Association)

Mann & Overton's catalogue for 1938. Even by then, the Taxi had yet to adopt the cowled radiator, this happened for 1939. Inside were illustrations of the two 1938 cabs which were available at that time, with Jones and Strachan bodywork respectively.

Mann & Overton's advert from The Steering Wheel, *the taxi trade magazine, of the early "high-loader" style cab.*

Loader chassis. Strachan bodies for the London General were identical to the normal Strachan coach work with the exception of the rear window in the cab's folding roof being oval rather than rectangular.

Vincents of Reading. A company founded in 1805 as builders of horse-drawn coaches and carriages. In 1899 they began to build the coachwork for motor cars, and in 1909 they added Rolls Royce to their list of customers. In 1912 they started to build vehicles for the transportation of horses and became renowned for the manufacture of high quality horse boxes. By 1930 Vincents became involved in the manufacture of taxicab bodies for Austin chassis, with their first being dubbed the "High Lot" because it was over 7ft (over 2.1 metres) in height.

By 1934 their bodies conformed to the normal Low Loading Cabs which were being manufactured by other companies, however their design differed from most by slightly flaring out the rear end in order to accommodate the spare wheel. This style of body was thus described as a "Fishtail", for which official approved had to be obtained by the Public Carriage Office in 1935. Vincent's final design was submitted in 1934, but approval was not granted until the June of 1936. This was designated the "Flash lot" – not by the company but by the cabbies themselves who thought it looked flashy compared to the more conventionally designed cabs. By comparison Jones Bros produced cabs with similar styling, but met with approval from the PCO.

GH 2362, a 1930 Vincent bodied High Loader taxicab. (Photo: Peter Matchan)

A Low Loader taxicab with coachwork by Vincent's of Reading as advertised by Mann & Overton in The Steering Wheel *of 10 November 1934.*

THE TWELVE AS A WORKHORSE

A 1934 Christopher Dodson cab re-creating a wartime AFS commissioned cab, towing a fire pump trailer. (Photo: Anthony Blackman)

Throughout this chapter the reader will have come across certain references to taxicab terminology or "Cabby Lingo" such as may be found under the section on the "Chinese" cabs. Cabbies themselves have been largely responsible for this as for instance the terms "Fishtail" and "Flash Lot". The early taxicabs were known as High Loaders but were often referred to as a "High Lot" or '"Piano Grand" as against the later Low Loaders or LLs, with the lower, cross-braced chassis introduced in 1933. Additionally a cabby who owned his own cab, in other words an owner-driver, was referred to as a "Musher", whereas one who was learning the "Knowledge" was a "Butterboy". A "Bilker" was a fare who failed to pay when leaving the cab and the taxi meter was often referred to as a "Jewish piano"!

War work

The life of a London taxicab was just ten years, after which, having covered the best part of a million miles, they were considered to be only fit for scrap. However, this ruling was put on hold when in 1939 the start of the Second World War saw many cabs, including those approaching the end of their working life being pressed into undertaking war work.

At the outbreak of hostilities there were over 6690 cabs licensed in London, and of those, 2452 were requisitioned by the Government for war work, and 2000 were assigned to the Auxiliary Fire Service (AFS) to serve alongside the regular fire brigade in fighting the many fires caused by enemy bombardment. The remaining 452 were used for civil defence purposes and by the Home Guard. But many taxicabs never made it through until the end of the War, as will be demonstrated by some of the following illustrations.

Cabs assigned to the fire service would be fitted with ladders secured to the roof racks, and a tow bar for pulling a trailer pump. Hoses and all other equipment required for fighting fires were stowed inside the cab and on the luggage area located next to the driver, in addition to which they also carried a crew of five or six regular fire fighters.

The taxicabs which were not conscripted, such as the 1932 "High Lot" GX 4716 shown above, carried on plying for hire. This photo of a cabby waiting on a rank somewhere in London was taken towards the end of the war. The owner obviously had difficulty in finding new tyres for his cab. The nearside headlamp has had the bulb removed whilst that on the offside is fitted with a regulation mask. (Photo of unknown origin)

Ready for action. This 1935 Jones-bodied cab complete with fire crew and all the equipment is ready for what the Luftwaffe may throw at them. (Photo: The London Fire Brigade)

This image shows how some of the equipment was stored inside the cab in addition to being carried in the luggage compartment next to the driver. (Photo: The London Fire Brigade)

An early High-Loader taxicab and crew of five fire fighters pose for a photograph outside their headquarters. (Photo: The London Fire Brigade)

Above: A side view of ALU 953 showing the extent of the damage caused by the falling masonry. (Photo: The London Fire Brigade)

ALU 953 an early (1933) High Loader flattened by falling masonry. Not very much could be salvaged from this wreck as even the front tyres were past their best! (Photo: The London Fire Brigade)

Far right: A line up of taxicabs severely damaged by a nearby bomb blast. (Photo: The London Fire Brigade)

THE TWELVE AS A WORKHORSE

Many of the requisitioned taxicabs were painted grey, but BYV 31 still seems to have retained its original two-tone livery. (Photo: The London Fire Brigade)

Not all cabs were requisitioned by the Fire Service. BXV 71, a 1934 Jones-bodied Low Loader is seen here in use by the Home Guard. For once, the hood was lowered! (Photo: the London Vintage Taxi Association)

EUW 349, a 1938 Low Loader, did not appear to be too badly damaged but the 1933 High Loader which was standing next to it would never ply for hire again. (Photo: The London Fire Brigade)

A 1939-40 "Flash lot" chassis fitted out as a 15cwt military truck. (Photo from the Austin Handbook publication number 1818 issued in 1939-40)

Oxford Circus circa 1952, with the pre-war Austin taxis nearing the end of their life, but the ones we see here are still looking to be in good condition.

BYX 306 a former London taxi now named "Salome", at Calais returning from a European adventure.

The owners of requisitioned cabs were retained to drive them, as they had a good knowledge of the London back streets and could probably reach the scene of a fire quicker than the regular fire brigade drivers. Drivers were paid £1 17s 6d (£1.875) per week for the use of their cabs and a further £3 for driving them.

Not only did the Austin Twelve-Four continue in production in taxi form several years after the private car had been discontinued in 1935, but the simple chassis and robust engine were considered ideally suited by the military to serve as light trucks. And so, in 1939-40 a remaining batch of taxi chassis were fitted instead with "utility" truck bodies for the military, under contract number 294/V/3747, for which Austin issued a special handbook publication number 1818.

By the end of hostilities there were fewer than 3000 cabs considered to be in a fit state to continue plying for hire, and with spare parts almost non-existent, those that survived just had to soldier on as best they could. It would be at least a further three or four years before any new taxicabs would be available, which saw those that had survived the war carry on serving the public well into the mid-1950s, when the oldest would have been on the road for 25 years.

A new life for some survivors

Once the war ended and new taxicabs began to make their presence felt, it was time for those which had served London so well for almost two decades to be retired, and indeed many hundreds ended their life being broken up for scrap.

In spite of their excessive mileage, a decent taxicab straight off the ranks could fetch anything up to £60, but most were sold on for considerably less than that, and for five to ten pounds they were snapped up by students and returning American servicemen, as a quaint old English reminder of their stay in the UK during the war. Students considered that owning an old taxicab was great fun, and having one opened up many adventures travelling abroad into war-torn Europe and beyond.

Les Davis was one such student who paid the full amount of £60 for his 1934 Low Loader (BYK 711), which he called "Clara", and then toured France, Germany, Austria and Switzerland with four of his friends. In spite of its age the cab performed very well and attracted a lot of attention wherever it was parked. On average they experienced at least one minor breakdown every day and suffered overheating when attempting to cross over the Julier Pass in Switzerland, which at its highest point reaches an altitude of 7493 feet (2284 metres).

Les kept the cab for several years following the trip abroad, but as he failed to get £30 for it when he

Clara in old age: her driver looks happy enough!

THE TWELVE AS A WORKHORSE

Left: Nita Marriott with members of the French Foreign Legion at Tamanrasset, Algeria. (Photo: S Gifford)

The Jones Bros bodied Low Loader taxicab shown here was converted into a flower stall named "The Flower Box" and was frequently seen parked up in London's Knightsbridge area. The hood had been replaced with a snazzy canopy and the owner had fitted a door where the luggage compartment had been. (Photo: Mike Worthington-Williams)

David Suchet as Hercule Poirot about to enter his hired taxicab. (Photo: Anthony Blackman)

The dust jacket of Michael Marriott's book about their journey. This is the original 1956 edition; a 1958 paperback edition omitted the taxi in favour of an artist's impression of the Marriotts and a rather racy blurb.

Earning their keep. Pre-war London taxicabs continue to be much in demand at weddings. AXW 304, a 1934 Jones bodied three-quarter landaulet, and BLM 942, a 1934 Jones bodied Low Loader. (Photo: Calvin Candy)

Regrettably, when found to be of no further use, many were just abandoned and left to rot, but believe it or not these remains were rescued from further decay and once more resemble what they started life as – a taxicab!

Yes. It is the same taxicab now totally rebuilt in the style of a Strachan Low Loader. (Photos courtesy of the late Viv Orchard)

made it but died under a tree in Tanout, just a couple of hundred miles before reaching their intended destination. The couple recounted their adventure in a book entitled *Desert Taxi* which is well worth looking out for in secondhand book shops, or on websites.

There were many examples of taxicabs being done-up as country cottages complete with hanging baskets of flowers and a thatched roof, public houses with appropriate signage for various brands of alcohol, and one even ended up at Bertram Mills Circus, painted red and yellow as a plaything for the clowns. Fortunately there were many examples saved by individuals or by motor museums, some of which now earn a good living with the film and television industry, and of course as a bridal carriage for weddings

A 1933 High Loader with the number plate DLT 141 (the real registration was actually ALE 165) played an important part in the filming of an episode of the *Poirot* television series. This taxicab came straight off the ranks and into preservation, and at one time was painted yellow! It is now restored to exactly how it should look.

"Peggy": A rather special taxicab

"Peggy" is a 1935 Strachan-bodied low-loader taxicab which has had quite an interesting life since leaving the ranks in the early 1950s. Registered as DYH 310 in 1935, the cab had its coachwork built as a knock-down kit for The London General Cab Company (LGC Co) by Strachan of North Acton. LGC Co, which had no connection with the London General Omnibus Company, was a major London cab operators. The kit was then assembled by the LGC Co at their Brixton works on an Austin Twelve-Four chassis which had been delivered to them direct from Longbridge.

advertised it for sale, he donated it to a friend who parked it in his garden for his children to play in. However it had not been there very long before its new owner was approached by the Scout leader of a group in Perivale, Middlesex, who requested it for transporting their camping equipment around.

One couple, Michael and Nita Marriott, purchased their 1935 Low Loader, CLD 532, which they called "Bertha" and attempted to drive it across the Sahara Desert and down to Kano in Nigeria. The cab almost

Far left: Charles Hawtree learning to drive "Peggy" in the film Carry on Cabby *with Sid James sitting in the luggage space next to the driver's seat. (Photo: Pinewood Studios)*

Left: Sid James and Hattie Jacques celebrate their nuptials over the bonnet of "Peggy". (Photo: Pinewood Studio)

The LGC Co was based at 1-3 Brixton Road, Brixton, in South East London and as well as operating their own fleet of taxicabs also had facilities for building them. However, they relied on established coachbuilders such as Strachan to supply knock-down kits for them to assemble. The London General cabs were therefore identical to those built at North Acton with just one small deviation. At the rear of the folding hood the Strachan built cabs had a small rectangular window, whereas those built for the LGC Co were oval.

Now back to DYH 310. When the time came to withdraw this particular taxicab from the ranks, it was decided to retain it in the company's "museum" where over the years they had assembled a few examples of early cabs which they often hired out to film companies. The cab was therefore in a very good condition and was always kept roadworthy.

In 1962 the London General was approached by the Peter Rogers film production company who were about to make a comedy film about two rival cab companies called *Carry on Cabby*, and they were looking for an early taxicab to play a major role as the taxi on which a learner driver cabby would cut his teeth.

For the film, the number plate was changed to PEG 1 and the name "Peggy", which was the name of the proprietor's wife, played by Hattie Jacques, was painted on the sides of the bonnet. Actor Charles Hawtree was the "Butterboy" (learner driver) who spent most of the time driving the cab in shot. The proprietor of the cab company was played by actor Sid James. The film was of course a resounding success and one of 32 *Carry-On* films to be released over the following thirty years.

Several years later the London General decided to sell off its collection of aged taxicabs and Peggy is now owned privately by a member of the Vintage Austin Register. Whilst still in the ownership of London General, the cab made appearances in several other films such as *The Battle of Britain* and *One of Our Dinosaurs is Missing*, to name just a couple.

"Peggy", the 1935 Strachan taxicab followed by another cab with the same coachwork. (Photo: Malcolm Tearle)

Now with its correct registration plate DYH 310. (Photo: Malcolm Tearle)

This photo was taken in 2018 at a Vintage Austin Register event at Chateau Impney, Worcestershire. (Photo: Malcolm Tearle)

Chapter Nine

STORIES FROM OWNERS, IN FACT AND IN FICTION

Those of us who have ever owned or driven a motor vehicle will be aware that at some time during its ownership they will have experienced an unexpected stoppage caused by a failure of a vital part. In my own experience of over fifty years of driving, I have endured the failure of a big-end bearing on a Ford Prefect and on an Austin Light 12/4; a detached prop shaft from a Ford Zephyr 4, a broken timing belt on an Austin Montego, a complete brake failure on a 1938 taxicab whilst holidaying in Guernsey, and the loss of the sunroof whilst driving at speed (well, sort of!) in a Morris Eight along Ealing Broadway. So this chapter is devoted to just a few of those stories where the "Dependable" Twelve-Four tended to prove otherwise. I commence this chapter with my own experience of one such occasion . . . .

Left in the lurch – like waiting for Godot

YU 4277 was a 1927 Windsor saloon, purchased back in the mid-1960s for the princely sum of £70. The car had not been on the road since the early 1950s and was in a parlous state. It had many of the roof timbers rotted, the steel scuttle had a large hole in the top, and the bottom edges were rusted away to just below to where the air vents began. However with youth on my side and enthusiasm by the bucket load I started work on its restoration.

When work was completed the Windsor looked superb once more. However my wife and I had always desired an open tourer and on finding someone with a Light 12/4 tourer who was willing to swap it for the Windsor, I readily agreed. The owner of the Light 12/4 lived some 50 miles away in West London, whilst the car he wished to exchange it with was down in Kent where I lived.

From subsequent telephone conversations, I was led to understand that the Light 12/4 would be brought down on a trailer, and the Windsor taken back the same way, which after all was the most sensible thing to do. So it came as rather a surprise to find that he had actually come in his modern car and intended to drive the Windsor back to Ealing with me following in his car, and then for me to drive the Light 12/4 back again.

At this point it has to be said that the Windsor was not insured or taxed and did not have and MOT certificate, and the furthest I had actually driven it was less than about half a mile – oh and the tyres were not in the best of condition either. All this was of no real concern to the new owner, though at this stage, as no paperwork had been exchanged, technically the car was still mine.

We then set off, and I could see that the Windsor was responding well and maintaining a steady 40-45mph along the A2, the main London to Dover trunk road, and I settled down to watching its progress with some

This shows some of the work undertaken to replace rotted metalwork, on the offside of the scuttle of YU 4277. (Photo by author)

satisfaction knowing that all my work on the engine had been successful. However that was to change: as we approached Bromley a puff of black smoke came out from the exhaust pipe and the car pulled over to the side of the road and stopped.

A quick examination showed that the magneto, which had not been in use for many years had decided that enough was enough, and had seized up. The new owner was not too perturbed, as he had a couple of spares back home and would shoot off and bring them back in no time at all, leaving me alone with the Windsor.

I suppose I had been sitting there for about 10 to 15 minutes when to my horror a police patrol car drove up and stopped directly in front of me. The car's two occupants came over and politely asked what the problem was, and whether or not I required any help.

They then both had a good look around the car, with me standing in front of the front nearside wheel in order to try and hide the lack of tread on its tyre. Fortunately they appeared more interested in the standard of work which I had achieved and did not seek to enquire as to whether it was taxed, insured or even roadworthy. Satisfied that I was OK and not requiring any further help, they bid me farewell and drove off.

Whilst waiting for the new owner to return I noted that the same police patrol went past me on five further occasions, each time the occupants giving a friendly toot and a wave as they drove past. It was over three and a half hours before the new owner returned with the replacement magneto, as he had decided to stop off for lunch on the way back.

However once the replacement magneto was fitted and the engine re-timed the Austin started up straight away and was able to complete its journey without any further mishaps. The Light 12/4 did not stay with me very long as the body tended to flex when going round corners causing the doors to fly open.

We have had enough of experts!

Calvin Candy had a similar experience to the one above when he went to collect a Burnham Saloon (VM 4112) for which he had just paid £1500. Calvin, not knowing much about Austin Twelves, had enlisted the help of a friend who apparently had experience with such motor cars, having once rebuilt a Twelve-Four Clifton tourer.

On arriving at the seller's address in Bognor Regis, and after handing over the asking price to the owner, Calvin was disheartened to find that the car did not actually run. This was a problem. In spite of the fact that the car had no insurance, road tax or MOT,

Above: A recent image of YU 4277 as it appears today, repainted from the original dark blue (Photo from author's collection, source unknown)

Left: VM 4112, Calvin Candy's Twelve-Four Burnham Saloon. (Photo: Calvin Candy)

Calvin's friend was more than happy to take a chance and drive it home for him.

The knowledgeable friend then proceeded to check various parts of the engine and found that the valves were sticking. This he attempted to rectify by hitting the valve springs with a hammer and a screwdriver whilst Calvin turned the engine over using the starter motor. Although very concerned by the method George was employing, Calvin considered that he must know what he was doing, and indeed after several attempts the valves were loosened and the engine burst into life.

Checking that there was an adequate supply of fuel in the tank they set off on their journey home with Calvin following on behind. They had only driven about a mile down the road when they came to a halt. On checking the carburettor it was found that it was empty, so a further check was made on the Autovac, which was also empty. George filled the Autovac with petrol which then ran freely down into the carburettor. Job done, they then proceeded on their way.

They had not driven more than five miles when once again the car came to a stop with exactly the same problem as before. The Autovac was filled up once more and all went well for a further five miles when it stopped again. This was to happen every five or so miles for the entire length of the journey home.

On one of these impromptu stops it just so happened that the place where the Austin chose to come to a halt was right next to where a policeman was walking his beat. George, having pulled up directly at the point where the officer was about to pass, jumped out of the car and quickly opened the bonnet to attend to the problem, which by now he had mastered to a very high degree. The policeman stopped, and out of curiosity started to give the Austin a good looking over, then asked if we needed any help, to which George replied that it was just a minor fault and that they would soon be on their way again. The Police officer, satisfied with that, wished them well and bid them good day before continuing on his beat.

It was only later, when Calvin became more familiar with the workings of the Autovac that he discovered that the fuel and vacuum connections had, at some time been reversed, which is not an easy thing to do as they both have different fittings and would appear impossible to get wrong. However, once they had been swapped over the car ran like a dream.

It has to be said that the friend's "expertise" was probably not quite as good as he had made out, as a fault such as this should have been spotted easily, especially as he had to remove and replace those connectors every time the top of the Autovac was removed.

Marriage breakdown, with a happy ending

The next story was submitted by Bob Kendall whose experience when transporting the bride and groom from the church to their reception was one which we all hope will never occur on such an occasion.

After buying his 1927 Austin Twelve-Four Windsor saloon, he decided that it would be fun to use it for wedding hire. What a great excuse to use the car, meet people and earn a few pounds into the bargain? Initially all went well with plenty of bookings coming in and the car behaving itself perfectly. The Austin was remarkably reliable but, inevitably, something was bound to go wrong, and fate caught up with him on one miserable, rainy day in the early summer of 2009.

Bob did not usually accept bookings that were too far from home but, on this occasion, he had been persuaded to travel to a wedding about 30 miles away. However he noticed a gentle humming noise as he went to collect the bride which was getting gradually louder, but as there was little which he could do about it he carried on, collected the bride and delivered her to the church – all in the pouring rain.

She was very unhappy as she emerged from the car, and Bob thought this was due to the fact that she had been imagining her wedding day for years and pouring rain hadn't played a part in her dreams. To help matters Bob held a large umbrella over her head as she walked through the churchyard with tears gently running down her face when he heard her whisper to her mother "I don't want to be here".

The rain did not abate during the ceremony so they couldn't have their photographs taken outside and it was too wet to release the white doves she had ordered. Everything was going wrong and Bob was not particularly looking forward to the 10 mile journey to the reception. But, when the couple emerged from the church, her mood had changed entirely, and he imagined that the pressure had been lifted from her shoulders and that she had come to terms with the weather, which allowed her now to relax.

That was just as well, because they had travelled only a few miles along a busy main road when a bearing in the back axle failed in quite a spectacular fashion. Stray pieces of metal had jammed themselves into the running gear and the back wheels had locked solid. To Bob's utter astonishment, the bride took it quite well. She put on the yellow high-visibility jacket that was kept in a trunk strapped to the luggage rack, asked to borrow a spanner and posed for photographs at the side of the road, pretending to fix the car. She was laughing and joking as she waved to the people stuck in the traffic jam that was rapidly building up behind them.

Bob quickly concluded that the car could not be repaired at the roadside and called for a rescue truck. Apologising profusely, he asked the groom to call

Robert Kendall's 1927 Windsor Saloon, SV 6634. (Photo: Robert Kendall)

for a lift, and as he did so, the coach carrying their guests arrived at the front of the queue of traffic but, instead of stopping for the stranded couple, the driver carried on, with the guests waving and laughing as they flashed past. "I don't believe they just did that" said the bride before dissolving into peals of laughter. Thank goodness her mood had changed so completely!

They eventually managed to get a lift from a passing guest, leaving Bob shivering beside the road awaiting the arrival of the recovery vehicle. He subsequently contacted the bride to apologise again and offered to return her money. She would have none of it, saying they would remember our adventures for years to come, and that the whole experience was well worth the money. Phew! What a relief.

Later, a replacement back axle was acquired, which was fitted without too much trouble and remains on the car to this day.

A passable hen house

For our next story, we go back to the days when, shortly after the end of the 1939-45 war, new cars were almost impossible to obtain and old secondhand ones were therefore very much in demand – that is, if you could get them! Michael Rabiger recounts the time when his parents purchased their Austin Twelve:

"My Austin memory concerns my mother in the late 1940s. My dad had started his own painting and decorating business after he was demobbed and, to begin with, he would set out on a gaunt black bicycle with two paint pots strapped to the luggage carrier. My mother meanwhile was prospecting for motorised wheels and she found a 1928 Austin in a farmyard going for a very reasonable sum.

"There was a catch, of course; it had been used as a hen house for the entire period of the war and was inches deep in foul-smelling chicken mess. Initially the car had to be emptied of its unwelcome contents, whereupon my dad became the proud owner of the most worn-out Austin in the Home Counties. All its tyres, on their artillery wheels, were paper thin, the brakes were worn-out, every bearing was on its last legs, and the pistons rattled in the block.

"Because he could not afford a new battery, the car had to be push-started. I would regularly see my dad and his assistant valiantly pushing it down the road and then jump in to engage the gears and try starting the worn-out engine. I got my introduction to engineering with Meccano and that car; I had the ideas and my dad had the strength to carry them out.

"There is one good family outing that I particularly remember. Being an open car, it was a pleasant experience to tour around the Buckinghamshire villages where we lived. On one occasion, as we returned home, there was an echoing explosion, like mortar-fire, that set all the village dogs barking. One of the front tyres was flapping a burst inner tube on the road but, luckily we were close to home and limped the final 100 yards on the rim. Sometime after this, my dad entered the film business as an apprentice make-up man and we graduated to a Wolseley Hornet, but I shall always have happy memories of the Austin."

The Rabigers' 1928 Clifton taken during in the winter of 1947, shortly after purchase. Note the missing headlamp, a replacement could not be found! (Photo: Michael Rabiger)

"Bluebell", John Wise's 1924 Clifton Tourer. (Photo: John Wise)

Breakdown at a funeral

When a breakdown occurs, it will usually happen when it is least expected, or in a location where you would rather it had not happened. Such was the situation when John Wise decided to drive his 1924 Clifton to a late friend's funeral from Waterlooville to Portchester. The car went well, as indeed an Austin should, but when the time came to leave the crematorium the car (known as "Bluebell"!) refused to start. Ironic, seeing where it was parked!

After having spent half an hour trying to fathom out why this sudden and unexpected failure had occurred without any success, there was nothing left to do but to ring the AA and arrange for it to be transported home.

When John began to investigate why "Bluebell" had let him down so badly, he started with the magneto, which on test proved to be providing only a very weak spark. The magneto was removed and sent off for repair and when returned it looked as good as new, and when bench tested it produced an enormous spark.

The engine was turned to top dead centre, and rotated to number one contact point, and then secured back in its place. Ignition on, engine rotated but apart from an intermittent back-fire – nothing! The magneto was removed for a second time and again bench tested, to discover that it produced a huge but intermittent spark which was certainly not a good sign.

Once the magneto returned to the repairers, John took the opportunity to check other parts of the engine and found that the Autovac, the device for providing fuel to the carburettor, was not working as well as it should. This led to the removal of the cylinder head and a thorough de-coke, where it was discovered that two of the exhaust valves were stuck in the open position. The valves were removed, cleaned and replaced and reground.

By this time the magneto had been returned with a note explaining that the reason for the intermittent spark was found to be due to a deficiency in what was a new contact set. This had now been replaced and the magneto worked once more exactly as it should.

Once the magneto had been refitted and the engine re-timed, the Austin started up immediately and now runs very well. The sticking valves were due to a couple of factors, one being that due to a serious health problem John had not used "Bluebell" for a couple of years, and secondly from 2015 to 2018 the engine was run too rich, which caused carbon deposits to build up around the exhaust valves. The nine-mile drive to the crematorium was its first outing in nine months, and seeing what problems were to be found on stripping down the engine, it is a wonder that it ever reached the crematorium!

No smoke without a fire

It is fair to say that not all breakdowns are due to failure of the car or its component parts, for occasionally a breakdown requiring a journey back home on the back of a breakdown truck may be solely down to something which the driver may have inadvertently caused. We now look at such an incident as related by Tom Stapleton.

Tom had arranged a day out for friends and family to enjoy a pleasant lunch at a lovely country pub located just outside Chester. Tom driving "Princess" his 1931 New Windsor saloon, with his wife and her brother following in their 1933 Austin 10/4.

It was New Year's Day and the weather could not have been nicer, and both cars were motoring along very well. Then Tom, looking in the rear view mirror, thought that the road behind him looked a bit hazy, and on taking a closer look noted that there was smoke coming from his car. Once parked safely at the roadside it was discovered that the handbrake had been left slightly on which had caused friction between the brake shoes and the brake drum which is a transmission brake located directly behind the gear box, and when applied prevents the prop shaft, and thus the rear wheels from rotating.

With the brake now released and the smoke subsided Tom decided that all was now well and proceeded on to the pub, a little late but at least he was on his way. He had not been driving for more than a couple of miles when he was aware that the car was struggling and not pulling at all well, once again flashing headlights indicated that yet again smoke was seen coming from under the Austin. Of course, generally speaking, where there's smoke there's fire and indeed that was the case with "Princess".

So on finding a convenient place to pull over, with smoke now billowing up inside the car and flames now clearly visible, serious measures had to be taken. Wisely Tom always kept a fire extinguisher in the car and this was quickly brought into use, whilst his brother-in-law brought the extinguisher from the Austin Ten.

However no matter how he tried, he could not get the extinguisher to work, and the gauge on the one from the Austin 10 showed "empty". At this point Tom decided to get technical and gave his extinguisher a hard bash on the kerbstone, a second bash did the trick and the fire was put out in seconds, which was just as well because that was as long as the extinguisher lasted to discharge its contents. With the carpet and floorboards removed it became obvious that the fabric coupling was still smoking and the brake drum still very hot.

At this point, a friend, who was also on his way to the pub in his Clifton tourer, stopped and brought over a container of water which, when applied to the seat of the fire cooled and neutralised the source of it. It was at this point that Tom suddenly remembered

"Princess", Tom Stapleton's 1931 New Windsor saloon. (Photo: Tom Stapleton)

the containers of water which he always carried, for drinking and putting out occasional fires!

Now that the car was considered safe to continue, they decided to carry on to the pub as planned, and with floorboards removed and a good airflow, an eye could be kept on the transmission brake – just in case! On this occasion the Austin did not require the services of a breakdown truck and their party arrived safely at the venue only 15 minutes late.

The journey home was without further incidents, except that any speed over 20mph caused very bad vibration from the prop shaft, and when it was eventually removed Tom found that the fabric coupling needed to be replaced at a cost of over £100, and several hours spent on his back underneath the car to replace it.

For want of a nut, the brakes were lost

This final tale occurred in 1980 when my wife and I decided to take a holiday in Guernsey, using our 1938 Low-Loader taxicab as our means of transport. As the children were of an age where sand and sea were important we set off one morning to find a suitable beach by travelling along the hilly coastline up and down hills looking out for a suitable spot to park.

When we came across a beach which we thought was ideal, the family were surprised to find that instead of parking up, I had continued driving on and away up the hill. What they were unaware of was that I could not have stopped because I actually had no brakes!

A nut had worked loose from a bolt connected to the braking system and effectively we had no means of being able to stop. Of course I did not let this little gem of information become known to my family and once reaching the top of the hill managed to bring the cab to a halt. Then, and only then, did I tell them why I had not stopped when asked. A replacement nut and bolt were found in the tool box and we were able to continue our holiday without further incidents.

Gumdrop: A very famous Austin Twelve

Gumdrop is the name of a 1926 Austin Twelve-Four Clifton tourer much revered by younger readers, many of whom are now grown up and have children of their own. It is considered that many of these youngsters actually began to read simply because of the books written and illustrated by its owner, the late Val Biro.

It was never Val's intention to purchase, an Austin Clifton tourer, but he came across it whilst on his way to view, and probably purchase a 1948 Rover which he had been told about. However, as he stopped for fuel at a garage in the village of Hardwick, he spotted a very old car parked at the rear of several others which were being offered for sale.

The taxi and Stringer family, plus my wife's sister and her husband who were on their honeymoon in Jersey and had decided to fly over to see what Guernsey was like! (Photo by author)

On enquiring about this motor car, he was told that it was being sold on behalf of the local scrap dealer who considered it to be too good to scrap, and had "done it up" to make it presentable to sell on. However he was advised that the engine might require some money to be spent on it as it was "on its last legs". So in 1961 and for just £100, Val was now the proud owner of a 1926 Austin Twelve-Four Clifton Tourer which his wife immediately named *Gumdrop*, after a 1933 Austin Seven which had previously been owned by him and which his wife had also named Gumdrop.

Once home, and the engine attended to, Gumdrop was to make several major journeys up to Scotland and down into Cornwall, and was considered to be so reliable that it was used as Val's normal everyday means of transport.

At that time Val was earning a living as an illustrator, designing book covers and occasionally covers for the *Radio Times*, and it was with regard to further work in this area that he drove up from his home in Buckinghamshire to Leicester to meet up with his agent Ewart Wharmby of the Brockhampton Press to discuss a prospective commission.

Over lunch the topic of conversation turned to Gumdrop during which Val was able to tell Ewart all about the car and just how much it meant to him. Ewart must have been very interested in Val's story as he suggested that if he wrote a book about the car

Val Biro's Gumdrop (Photo: Mike Hodgson)

Val Biro at work. (Photo: the Enid Blyton Society)

The cover of the first Gumdrop book.

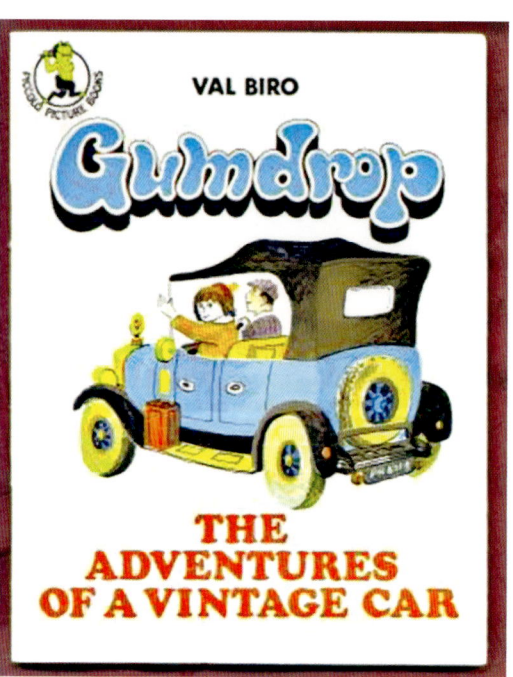

Mr Josiah Oldcastle, one of the characters which appeared in many of the Gumdrop books. (Illustration courtesy of the late Val Biro)

Sir Bernard Miles seated in Gumdrop at the Thames Television Studios. (Photo: the late Val Biro and author's collection)

Starting Gumdrop on the handle. Taken in 2005 at Cofton Park near Longbridge on the occasion of the Austin Centenary Rally. (Photo by author)

aimed at young children, he would certainly consider it for publication.

Val's thoughts on ideas for such a storybook occupied much of the journey home, and it was not long before he was back again in Leicester to submit what he had written to Ewart. His story, *Gumdrop – The Adventures of a Vintage Car* was duly published in 1966 and very well received. The following year a second book was written entitled *Gumdrop – The Farmer's Friend,* which like the previous book was also a success, and even attracted the attention of the BBC who thought it would be rather good to adapt for *Play School* using the actual vehicles mentioned in the book.

Not long afterwards ITV's Thames Television contacted Val with a proposal that Sir Bernard Miles should read one of the Gumdrop stories. To this he agreed and Val of course took Gumdrop along to the studio. Once Sir Bernard had decided what type of voices he should use in the telling of the story, the broadcast went live on air and, like the books themselves, was a complete success.

In a later book, *Gumdrop on the Brighton Run,* which was launched on the first Sunday in November when the London to Brighton Run is always held, Val was given permission by the RAC, organisers of the event, to allow Gumdrop to be parked along the Madeira Drive together with the arriving Veteran cars. It should be noted that in the story, Gumdrop had been given the title "An Honorary Veteran Extraordinary".

By now the Gumdrop books had become established as easy reading for children, and encouraged those who had never read before to pick up a Gumdrop book as their first approach to reading. Val also agreed to take Gumdrop to a local primary school to read one of his stories to the children. This of course led to Gumdrop being driven further and further to satisfy requests for public appearances, totting up an average of over 6000 miles every year.

Val Biro was to write a further 36 books featuring his well-known and much loved 1926 Austin Clifton tourer. *Gumdrop's School Adventure* was the final Gumdrop story and was written and published in 2001. Sadly, on 4 July 2014, at the age of 94, Val passed peacefully away.

Chapter Ten

SURVIVORS AND LOSERS: TWELVES ADAPTED, REBORN, OR DESTROYED

A few unusual uses for the Twelve

The Austin Motor Company used many catchy slogans when promoting its products, such as: "You Buy a Car but You Invest in an Austin", or "The Dependable Austin". But no-one in the publicity department seems to have considered that the Twelve-Four could perhaps be used for purposes other than to transport family and friends in comfort. In the following we look at some unusual adaptations or uses of Austin Twelves.

In or around 1927 the New South Wales Railway Company purchased several open touring cars for transporting the employees' wages. In August 1927 Austin had widened the track of the Twelve-Four from 4ft 4in to 4ft 8in which corresponded rather well to the railway track gauge of 4ft 8.5in. All that was required was to change the wheels, oh, and perhaps locking the steering!

The next photograph shows "Strong Man" Wilfred Briton from Leeds in Yorkshire supporting the weight of a 1928 Windsor Saloon on his back. The car weighed just under a ton, and it beggars belief how it was actually placed there. One interesting point was the radiator muff being still in place when the photograph was taken on 13 July 1934. Wilfred was acclaimed

Mr Wilfred Briton really putting his back into the job. (Photo from the Manchester Daily Mail)

Far left: Austin Twelve-Four adapted for use on the railway. (Photo from the Sydney Morning Post)

Left: De Maschio's Austin Ice Cream van. (Photo: the SCHVPT)

A 1930 Twelve-Four converted to a rather homely motor caravan. (Photos courtesy of Anthony Mealing)

Below: 1927 Twelve-Four Ambulance, with the Wellington Town Hall just visible in the background, and the interior of the ambulance. (Photos courtesy of the Alexander Turnbull Library, New Zealand)

as "Britain's Strongest Man" and during the 1930s demonstrated this by hauling a fully laden coach, a double-deck bus, and various lorries with his teeth!

The rather ornate ice cream vendor's van featured in the next photograph was commissioned by a Mr De Maschio. It was based on a 1930 Austin Twelve-Four chassis and built by Gibson & Brown of Tunbridge Wells, where the De Maschio Ice Cream business was based. The van was purchased at auction in 1981 by the Southern Counties Historic Vehicle Preservation Trust.

Sold recently at auction, this superb Austin motorised caravan was originally built in 1930 as an ambulance and later converted to act as a control vehicle at a Dublin airfield where it subsequently stood abandoned for a number of years. From there it was rescued and then re-built as it appears today. It will be noted that the vehicle features the most unusual slightly curved front doors. The coachbuilder is regrettably not known.

The next example to demonstrate the Austin Twelve's adaptability is this 1927 ambulance in a photo taken prior to delivery to the Wairarapa Hospital Board, in Wellington, New Zealand. It is not known whether the body was made by a UK coachbuilder such as Startins of Birmingham who, as well as hearses and Austin Seven van bodies, also built many ambulances, but since most new cars were exported to New Zealand in chassis form, it is perhaps more likely to have been built locally (see also chapter 5).

There have of course been many other examples of conversions, such as farm tractors, ambulances and even hearses, but those featured above are just a few which illustrate what the Austin Twelve-Four was capable of being adapted to.

By the late 1950s, many aged Austin Twelves were either sent to the breaker's yard or adapted to perform other roles, such as this one seen here helping out collecting the hay on a farm in Somerset. This Clifton, cunningly disguised as a mobile haystack, would have been just over thirty years old when the photograph was taken.

And finally, a 1927 Clifton tourer towing a caravan seen here parked at the roadside for a photograph, prior to reaching a suitable spot for a camping holiday. This picture has been included simply to illustrate a typical use for the Twelve-Four which Sir Herbert may well have intended.

Some Austin Phoenixes

In much the same way as the Phoenix, a mythical bird which, after being consumed by fire, was re-born from the ashes, so too have there been many an Austin motor car, taxi, truck or van which has been returned to the road after being left to rot in a field, or abandoned in a barn or garage over a period of many years.

Normally, these vehicles would have been scrapped or just left where they were, but those with a sharp eye, very deep pockets, and enthusiasm by the bucket load, could see an abandoned Austin Twelve-Four as a golden opportunity to resurrect one of Herbert Austin's forgotten and unloved motor cars, and to put it back on the road again where it belongs.

This chapter features just a few examples of Austin Twelve-Fours which have thankfully, like the Phoenix, been brought back to life again. We commence with the case of the New Zealand Post Office Van.

The 1930 Post Office van

On 20 June 1930, in Palmerston North, the New Zealand Post and Telegraph department registered one of several Austin Twelve-Four light delivery vans. The van had been shipped over from the UK as a complete running chassis; and then had its bodywork constructed at the Post Office workshops, which were located on the Wellington waterfront. As this work was carried out on the third floor of the workshop, it meant that the vans had to be taken up there using a very large electric lift.

Chassis such as these had been imported through the New Zealand Government's Stores Board since 1922 and they came complete with mudguards, bonnet and cowl, but unlike those intended to be bodied simply as cars the cowls on the van chassis did not have scuttle vents and the rear springs were supplied with twelve leaves instead of the usual ten.

After several years of Post Office usage, the van was eventually sold on, and, following a quick repaint in light green, it continued to give its new owner excellent service. The van was used throughout the war and as petrol was heavily rationed, it was run with a gas producer unit strapped to the near-side running board: however this proved not to be such a good idea as it set light to the grass on the side of the road as the van was being driven along.

In 1951, the van was sold to a farmer who converted it into a flatbed farm truck. He painted it dark blue and fitted small doors which he painted silver. He then sold it on to a young lad who used it to convey his friends every Saturday night to the cinema in Mangaweka a distance of almost 9 miles from where he lived in Rangawahia.

In the late 1950s, the next owner, another farmer named John Oakden, used it primarily to transport potatoes and fence posts. Chains were attached to the rear wheels to provide better traction. John's dog was a regular passenger and always sat next to the driver

"The Haywain". (Photo: Roger Fox)

A 1928 Clifton Tourer towing an early caravan and after setting up camp. (Photos courtesy of the Vintage Austin Register Archive)

The New Zealand Post Office van converted to a flatbed truck (Photo: Dennis Milne).

Abandoned and derelict. (Photo: Dennis Milne)

What the van would have looked like when it was new in 1929. (Photos courtesy of The New Zealand Postal History Society)

The Royal Mail van back on the road again, but now fitted with doors. (Photos courtesy of Dennis Milne)

whenever they went out, but when John got married, the dog refused to give up its seat, so his wife had to travel in the back of the truck seated on sacks. John kept the Austin for many years and when it had out-lived its usefulness he parked it under a large macrocarpa tree on his farm where it was left to slowly rot away.

Forty-five years later in February 2000, John retired and sold his farm. The remains of the truck were obtained by the present owner, Dennis Milne, who found that the years had not been kind to the vehicle, as it had been partially crushed by branches which had fallen from the tree. It took several days to remove, using a chainsaw to cut away the branches and a tractor to pull it clear. All the rotted timber from the vehicle was collected together and set aside to use as patterns.

The original idea behind owning this vehicle was either to restore it as a light open-back truck or use it for spares which would go towards the restoration of a 1927 Austin Twelve-Four tourer, but on receiving the vehicle's paperwork, he was intrigued to discover that the Austin had actually started life as a Royal Mail delivery van, and decided that in view of this, and the fact that traces of red paint had been found on the windscreen posts, his efforts should be directed towards restoring it back to that. The problem now was to find out just what the vans had looked like, as there were no other surviving examples to go and look at.

A letter sent to the New Zealand post office was forwarded on to the Postal History Society whose response was that they did not hold out any hope of finding photographs or indeed any other information which would have helped in its restoration. There then followed several years of research into what the van would have originally looked like and also obtaining parts to replace those which were either beyond repair or just missing.

Wheels needed to be sought as those on the vehicle had sunk into the ground and rotted, but they still had the chains fitted! When the engine was removed and sent away for overhaul, the clutch plates were exposed which revealed the reason why the van was abandoned, as the linings were worn out and the parts which remained were soaked with oil, and the plates showed blue marks from overheating which had occurred as a result.

However several weeks following their earlier response a further letter was received from the Postal History Society containing two photographs of a van built in May 1929 and one built in October 1930, and that the one built in 1929 had a long cowl, a fat radiator shell, early pattern wings and no doors, the 1930 van had a short cowl, thin radiator shell, later pattern wings and still no doors. The cost? £247.

Now, armed with this vital information work was able to commence in building the bodywork. Work carried out by previous owners had involved several modifications which all needed to be put back to how it was originally made.

On completion, permission then had to be obtained from the Post Office to use the logo which was in use during the early 1930s. The response was now very enthusiastic, and permission was readily granted, but, they advised that the logo chosen was not correct for that time and that the correct one would be made available to them. The work had taken just over five years to complete. The restored van runs well and attracts much admiration wherever it is parked.

The 1928 Windsor saloon

The next Phoenix Austin had spent over 30 years in a scrap yard, and when finally rescued changed hands several times until it was eventually purchased in or around 2010 by a Leicestershire couple who set to work in restoring it. On completion, the Austin was sold to someone in Ireland, but was returned in 2015 when it was purchased by the present owner.

The 1930 Special Two-four seater

The 1930 Special is one of only seven known to have survived from a batch of 50 manufactured between

The 1928 Windsor Saloon in the early stages of restoration after spending 30 years in a scrap yard. (Photos courtesy of Brian Porter)

The same car following extensive restoration work. (Photo: Brian Porter)

Far left: The 1930 Special as found. (Photo: Stephen Postlethwaite)

Left: The same car, now restored back to what it should be. (Photo: Stephen Postlethwaite)

1928 and 1930, and this fine example was purchased by Maurice Blake from its first owner, Flight-Lieutenant Slater, back in 1952. After he had driven the car home, Maurice put it away in his garage and never used it again, until following retirement in 1992, he began work on its restoration.

At that time the car was painted in a revolting shade of brown, the front bench seat was from something else and the dickey seat, whilst complete, was very battered. Restoration was completed during the year 2000, and five years later the car was driven to Birmingham's Cofton Park to attend the Centenary event of the Austin Motor Company which took place in July 2005.

1925 Clifton: The general condition of the scuttle and the wooden former which was used to shape the new scuttle. (Photo: Peter Moyle)

Below: Restoration completed, TT 3368 is now back on the road again. (Photo: Peter Moyle)

The 1925 Clifton Tourer

In 1970, Peter Moyle purchased the remains of a 1925 Clifton Tourer. Whilst the car was complete, it had suffered from serious neglect over the years and required more than just a little "TLC" to bring it back to life again. Peter commenced with the removal of the engine which he noted was stamped 1929, so at some time in its life the original short-stoke unit had been replaced. He decided to retain this later engine so it was stripped down and a considerable amount of work carried out before it was re-assembled, and declared capable of powering the Austin once again.

Then, due to family and work commitments any further work on the car came to a halt until early 2000, when, with more time available, Peter was able to look at what other work needed to be undertaken, which was considerable! What remained of the bodywork was removed from the chassis, which was then sand-blasted and repainted. Sand blasting of the petrol tank revealed several holes along the bottom, so this had to be cut out and a new base welded in place. Work needed to be carried out on the bodywork included new panels and doors and the scuttle which had almost rotted away.

There then followed restoration and overhaul of many of the ancillary parts, such as the magneto, Autovac, dynamo and the carburettor, whilst the bright parts such as the windscreen surround and radiator shell were sent away for re-plating. The spring sets of all seats needed replacing and then rebuilding, after which work on re-upholstering commenced using new horsehair, calico and brown crocodile patterned leather hide, which had to be specially made by a firm in Chesterfield which used the heated rollers originally used by Connolly's, the company which for many years supplied Longbridge with leather. The car is now finally completely restored and back on the road again, after last being used (according to the tax disc found in the licence holder) in 1951.

The London taxicabs

Anthony Blackman has long since been associated with pre-war London taxicabs and his interest and knowledge on them is second to none. His interest

1925 Clifton: The general condition of the scuttle and the wooden former which was used to shape the new scuttle. (Photo: Peter Moyle)

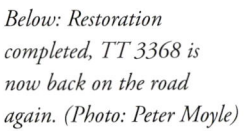

Below: Restoration completed, TT 3368 is now back on the road again. (Photo: Peter Moyle)

started back in 1962 when, as a young lad delivering newspapers he witnessed a 1936 Low Loader taxicab being dumped by the side of the road. Curiosity got the better of him and he cycled back to have a better look at what had just been abandoned. A few days later an "Abandoned" ticket had been stuck on the vehicle's windscreen by the council and this was seen as the right moment for Anthony to take positive action if the cab was to be saved.

Returning with the battery from his father's Hillman Minx and a set of jump leads made from flex salvaged from an old Goblin vacuum cleaner, several unsuccessful attempts were made to get it started, so with the help of some school friends the cab was pushed to his home, and thus began Anthony's obsession with pre-war London taxicabs.

By the mid-1980s, Anthony had built up a small collection of Austin cabs, a couple of which were in a very poor state of repair. One had been used by a group of hippies, whilst another had been employed as a tow vehicle for a cricket club's gang mower. In 1986 Anthony decided it was time to rebuild these two cabs and in order to do this, he decided to enrol for evening classes at Maidstone Technical College where he would have access to the best tools and facilities and expert tuition.

The first term was devoted to making the framework for both the bodies, the second and third to the panel work and then the wings. All this must have seemed very odd to the other students, who were making hat stands, coffee tables and table lamps – especially as the cost of £100 which Anthony was required to pay for all the items he had made was the same as that charged for a coffee table! The following year he joined the metalwork class and made the wings and body panels.

On one of its first outings to a vintage car rally, an elderly spectator gripped the edge of the front wing and, giving it a hearty lift, commented that "They don't build them like that anymore." Anthony did not have the heart to tell the gent that it was made in Maidstone in 1987.

ALN 281 was built in 1933, with coachwork by Jones Bros of Westbourne Grove, West London. In the early 1960s it was bought by a group of hippies who painted it yellow and embellished it with black spots. It came complete with window boxes, lavatory fittings and Ladies, Gentlemen and Pull to Flush type signs. The cab was originally owner-driven and was fitted out with several special extras such as deep pile carpet in the passenger compartment instead of the coconut matting. As explained in chapter 8, an owner-driver was also known as a "musher".

ALN 281 in process of being restored, and as completed with replica Jones Bros coachwork. (Photos courtesy of Anthony Blackman)

AXL 464 as found and as completed after a total rebuild. (Photos courtesy of Anthony Blackman)

HERBERT AUSTIN'S HEAVY TWELVE-FOUR 1922–39

PR 6079 has become a smart and usable drop-side truck, but which of those petrol cans has the whiskey in? (Photo: James Gray)

RK 7348 is now a light delivery van which was built to original coachbuilder's drawings. (Photo: James Gray)

1930 Austin Twelve-Four, car number 6TT 310, as found and after restoration. (Photos courtesy of Denis Le Cren)

AXL 464 was built a year later in 1934, and, like the cab above was also a High Loader fitted with Jones Bros coachwork. This cab was discovered in Cleveland where its bodywork had been removed back in 1958 to be used by a local cricket club to pull a gang mower around the grounds. The Taxi was originally operated by WH Cook & Sons.

A truck and a light delivery van

To conclude this section we take a look at two Austin Twelve-Fours which both started life as saloons in 1926. PR 6079 was reputed to have been on display at the Olympia Motor Show on the Austin stand in 1925 as a running chassis. After the show closed, the chassis was sent to Mulliners of Birmingham where it was fitted with a smart four-door coachbuilt saloon body. PR 6079 survived in rather poor condition until 1966 when a new owner, Mr ED Woolley, attempted to restore it. It eventually ended up with a car dealer in Manchester. Then, without its coachwork, the car went across to Ireland, where it was re-built as a drop-side truck. Whilst being used as a truck, the owner had converted a 2-gallon petrol can to conceal a bottle of Black Bush Irish Whiskey and two glasses. They are still carried even today on one of the running boards.

The second Twelve-Four, RK 7348, also started life in 1926 as a saloon finished in Maroon and Black and purchased by Mr Arthur Edmund from Croydon, and after several owners it ended up with a Mr Nigel Brake in Mid-Glamorgan. When purchased by the present owner, the vehicle was in a very poor state of repair, so it was decided to restore it as a light delivery van. The recreation took place over a nine-year period and was based on contemporary photographs and body-builder's drawings.

The last two photographs are of an Austin Twelve-Four tourer which was imported into New Zealand on 2 May 1930, and purchased by its Nelson owner for £375. Over the years the Austin became neglected and it was purchased by its present owner in the condition seen in the first photograph. Eighteen months later, following extensive restoration work the Austin was back on the road again, and for its first trip out covered a distance of over 124 miles without any problems.

Rust in peace!

Over the years, especially since the establishment of The Vintage Austin Register in 1958, which significantly raised awareness of the Austin Twelve's desirability as a practical and reliable vintage motor car, many examples have been brought back to life again. However, it is doubtful whether those which appear in this section ever did!

Whilst road accidents certainly accounted for many fine examples of the Austin Twelve failing to enjoy a long and happy life, it must also be said that the air raids inflicted upon London and other major cities by the Luftwaffe during the Second World War also played a significant part in preventing many from still being around today. The few examples shown here may have been used as donors to help others keep running, especially with regard to the taxicabs, for which tyres and spare parts were becoming increasingly hard to obtain as the war progressed.

Another culprit was of course the introduction of the MOT test in 1960-61, originally known as the "ten year test" which weeded out many elderly vehicles which perhaps today may have been considered to be worth saving, but instead sent them to an early grave.

The Harley all-weather coupé in the next photograph must have been hit by something going at quite a speed to have caused this amount of damage. It must have been a total write-off.

The untimely demise of this 1933 High Loader taxicab can be solely attributed to the Luftwaffe when one of its bombers chose to use it and the surrounding area for target practice during the 1939-45 war. (Photo: the London Fire Brigade)

It is understood this 1927 Windsor saloon came into contact with a heavily laden coal lorry. It rather looks like there is a bag of coal hanging from the driver's door handle.

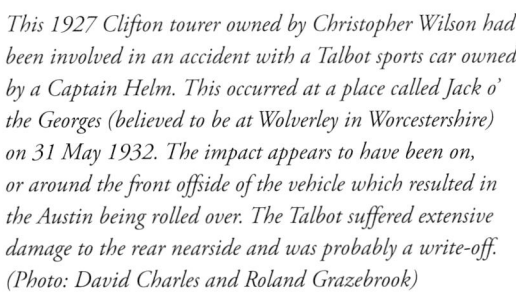

This 1927 Clifton tourer owned by Christopher Wilson had been involved in an accident with a Talbot sports car owned by a Captain Helm. This occurred at a place called Jack o' the Georges (believed to be at Wolverley in Worcestershire) on 31 May 1932. The impact appears to have been on, or around the front offside of the vehicle which resulted in the Austin being rolled over. The Talbot suffered extensive damage to the rear nearside and was probably a write-off. (Photo: David Charles and Roland Grazebrook)

Another case where well-worn tyres could have been the cause of an accident. The Twelve-Four saloon shown in this photograph was featured in an advertisement for Triplex Safety Glass in the May 1930 edition of The Austin Magazine. Apparently the car had been involved in a collision with a five-ton lorry. The windscreen, as can be seen, remains intact, other than an area where presumably the front seat passenger's head had come into contact with it. In their advert, Triplex commented that the consequences of the accident could have been far more serious, had the windscreen been fitted with "ordinary" plate glass. Of course, the accident may not have happened at all, had there been some tread on the front tyres. (Photo: The Vintage Austin Register magazine).

How this Caernarfon registered Austin saloon car (CC 684) came to be in the position it is shown here will probably never be known, but the driver probably got too close to the edge of the road. Like the other Austins shown in this section it too is unlikely to have been driven again. (Photo: North Wales Transport, *by Jim Roberts)*

Judging by the general condition of this 1928 Austin saloon, with no perceptible tread on any of the tyres, and dents probably caused by previous mishaps, it would appear that this encounter with 8 tons of City of Coventry Maudslay Omnibus in the Chapelfields area of Coventry sometime in the mid-1930s may have put it "beyond economical repair". The Austin appears to have come from Staffordshire and may be the driver was not used to city traffic… however it does appear to have been parked by the roadside, and maybe the driver of the bus misjudged the amount of room required to pass it!
(Photos courtesy of Victor Pettifor)

Sadly it is highly unlikely that this very early example of the Twelve-Four will ever run again – but who knows? Though not destroyed in the true sense of the word, this two-four seater dates from 1922 and can be viewed at the National Trust Property Erddig House, in Wrexham, together with a veteran Rover Eight and another Austin Twelve-Four. Technically this car appears to be in a very restorable condition – and it is probably the earliest Austin Twelve in existence, note the wooden wheels and one-piece front wings. The car next to it on the left appears to be a Clifton tourer, and is in good condition. Their owners, The National Trust, will not allow these cars to be brought back to original condition, and they are therefore unlikely to ever run again. Instead, they are to be maintained in the condition that they were left by the last eccentric private owner of the house. (Photo: the Vintage Austin Register Archives)

Appendix

The numbers which identify your Austin

The Austin Twelve-Fours have three identification numbers:

– A chassis number which ran in one continuous series from 101 in 1922 to well over 82000 in 1939-40, including taxi and WD utility vehicles, so this number will immediately identify the correct date of the car.

– A car number which was allocated in different series with different prefixes depending on the type of body. Furthermore, the prefix was changed to reflect major design changes over the years. The car number series (but not the chassis number series) were shared with the 16/6 models from 1927, as the bodies were the same or similar for the two models, but on the 16/6 the car number was suffixed with /6 or -6.

– An engine number, which like the chassis number ran in one series from start to finish. The engine numbers tend to be a little higher than the chassis numbers.

On the early Twelves, the "car number" was stamped on a circular plate measuring 2⅝in (67mm) in diameter, and this would be found either on the left hand side of the dashboard or mounted on the passenger door pillar.

On later cars, there are two small aluminium plates secured one above the other on the front of the bulkhead, above which will be found a third stating 'ALWAYS QUOTE THIS NUMBER'.

These were replaced in 1926 by the two rectangular plates of the type shown below, marked "Chassis" and "Car No", which are stamped with the numbers which will identify what type of car it is, and provides a clear indication of when it was built. Tony Smallbone, the Vintage Austin Register's restoration and technical secretary, explains what information these plates reveal.

The first Austin 12hp production cars, manufactured in early 1922, were either two-seaters or four-five seater tourers on a 4ft (1219mm) track chassis and these were allocated car numbers beginning with the prefix letters TT, which stood for "Twelve Touring". The model proved to be a success and the Company was soon unveiling improvements and upgrades. Notably amongst these was the widening of the track in October 1922, to 4ft 4in (1321mm) which prompted the introduction of an extra prefix character, the number 2. So a car bearing number 2TT 1234 would be a 12hp touring car with a 4ft 4in track.

Circular identification plate.

The chassis and car number identification plates. The plates shown are actually from a Sixteen-Six but the plates are of the same type as found on the Twelve-Four.

In 1923, the Harley All-Weather Coupé was added to the range, followed by the Windsor Saloon. On these cars the two letters of the car number were changed from TT to TC, the TC indicating "Twelve Closed". Another major change to the specification came about in September 1924 when front wheel brakes were introduced. At this point, the Company changed the prefix of the car number from 2 to 3. Until then, the letters had been restricted to either TT or TC, as previously described, but in 1924, TS came into use to identify the car as having a "Twelve Special" body, built by an outside coachbuilder such as Mulliner, Startin, Hoyal or Gordon. Where the coachbuilder was known to the Company, a further letter was inserted to indicate who that was, so if it happened to be Mulliner the Numbers would read: 3TS-M 1234. The numbers following the M would be those added by the coachbuilder.

In September 1924 the name Clifton was adopted for the touring car, but the car number prefix stayed as TT, as it did also on the later Open Road model.

The next major change occurred in September 1926 with the introduction of the long-stroke engine. The prefix of the car number then became 4 to identify this, but the vehicles still came with the 4ft 4in track. This series proved to be short-lived, lasting only to August 1927. The next series, bearing the prefix 5, came about when the track was widened to 4ft 8in (1422mm) and the height of the radiator cowl was raised. The two main body styles, tourer and saloon predominated so the majority of car numbers were prefixed 5TT or 5TC but now the car number could be also be prefixed TF which signified that the car had a fabric body.

The 6-prefix series was announced in late 1929, when a longer bonnet, a shorter scuttle, one-piece wings and chromium plating were all unveiled by the Company. There were numerous changes in design and mechanical features between late 1929 and 1933 but none were considered significant enough to justify the creation of another prefix. The first three characters or prefix of the car number are arguably of more interest than the remainder. The residual numbers identify the individual car and tell us little about the vehicle, other than giving an approximate indication of when, in the series, it was made. It should be mentioned that car numbers with the suffix /6 or -6 (see example above) signified a Sixteen six cylinder car introduced in October 1927. The prefix letters TT, TC, or TF remained the same, because the chassis was the same as the Twelve-Four.

This series continued through to 1933 when the 6TT, 6TC and 6TF prefixes were abandoned in favour of three-letter prefixes under which the various Twelve-Four body types were designated as follows (see also chapter 4 on standard body styles).

Prefix	Model name	Description	Production period	Notes
BPE	Harrow	9ft 4in wheelbase, two-seater	Dec 1933 to 1935	
BRN	Carlton (or Iver)	10ft wheelbase, six-light saloon	Dec 1933 to Jul 1934	Iver with division
BSF	Open Road	9ft 4in wheelbase, tourer	Dec 1933 to 1935	
BWN	Westminster	9ft 4in wheelbase, four-light saloon	Dec 1933 to Dec 1934	
BWQ	Westminster	9ft 4in wheelbase, four-light saloon	Feb 1935 to Apr 1936*	Cowled radiator
BRT	Berkeley	9ft 4in wheelbase, six-light saloon	Dec1933 to Jul 1934	
BRP	York	10ft 4in wheelbase, six-light saloon	Aug 1934 to Apr 1936*	Cowled radiator
BRU	Hertford	9ft 4in wheelbase, six-light saloon	Aug 1934 to Apr 1936*	Cowled radiator
BTH	Chalfont	10ft 4in wheelbase, six-light saloon	Aug 1935 to Apr 1936*	Cowled radiator; division

*The end date of April 1936 was quoted by RJ Wyatt but may be questionable.

From 1933 onwards, the 16 and 18hp six-cylinder models used similar prefixes but the first letter was E, so for instance an Eighteen York had a car number prefix of ERP, and their car numbers were then suffixed either 16 or 18 for the engine horsepower rating. A complete list of changes follows.

Significant changes from 1922 to 1938

Date	Chassis no. (or Engine no.)	Car no.	Modification
1922 Oct	1096	-	Petrol gauge
	1313	2TT 1026	4ft 4in track; First 2TT/TC car was 984, general production 1085 on 6 Nov 1922
1923 May	3200	2TT 2225	Dynamo coupling
1923 May	3189-3315		Engine: some with special pistons and rings
Aug	3976	2TT 2900	Steering lever inside front wings
1924 Jul	7246-8422		Engines, some with Coventry gears
Sep- Oct	8128	3TT 4986 3TT 5496 3TC 2201	First 3TT was 4986 in Sep, general production from 5496 on 10 Oct – four wheel brakes
Sep	8162	3TT 5800	Tappets
Oct	8254-8260	3TT 5900	Diff. piston centre
1925 Feb			Rear axle tube and adjustment covers
Mar	19732		Greasers
Sep	15199		Crankcase, main bearings, oil pipe, camshaft
Sep	15620	3TT 10629	Brake drums, universal joints

Nov	16954-17851		Battery box, frame member
	17014		Metaligators (metal covers for road springs)
Dec		3TC 5000	RA saloon
1926 Mar	18000-19000		Hertford shock absorbers changed to Smiths
Mar	18501		Steering column felt bushes
May	20353-20453		Ring type horn switch
Jun	21293-21821		Steering cross tube ends
Jul			Battery and casing 6 volt Lucas
Sep	23759		9:45 ratio
Sep	23983	3TT 15831	S tourer Nov
Sep-Oct	23919 or 24251;	4TT 15849	4T series with long-stroke engine
	Eng no 24400	4TC 6921	
		4TS 3592	
Sep	24078	4TT 15815	NB tourer
Nov	24305	4TS 3770	Lucas 12 volt system; first used on export cars in Feb 1927
		4TC 7240	
Nov	25228	4TT 16144	As above
1927 Jan	27940;		Crankcase, crankshaft, clutch cover
	Eng no 28163		
Feb	29490		Brake shoes and springs
Mar	30607		Petroscope
	30894		Rear axle bumper
Jun	35800;		Clutch springs
	Eng no 36000		
Jul	36154		Clamping nut and oil retaining ring
Aug	37179	5T series	Cowl raised, 4ft 8in track frame, air strangler cable
Nov	Eng no 40800		Valve springs
	40570		HT cable tube
1928 Jan	42426		Rear axle bumper
	43750		Grease gun adaptors
Feb	Eng no 45000		Oil tray and reservoir
Mar/Apr	45700		Bolt for flywheel cover
	46251		3-bracket step board
	46600-46800		Springs with zinc interleaves and gaiters
	46878		Battery box
May	47590		Exhaust pipe silencer tail pipe
	49551		Steering box bracket
Jul	40646 approx.		Springs
	49801		Larger petrol tank, 10 gallon capacity, and new gauge
	50125		Cross tube swivel arm
	50247		Heavy service tyres
	50450		Battery box tee bolt fixing
	50696		Colonial front springs and bumper
	50772		30in by 5in tyres
	51007/8. 51061/2		Valance fixed to frame
	51298		Strengthened frame
	52174		Head lamp single dipper

Nov			Larger steering wheel
	52859		Tank with dipper and plug
	53186		Reading light on instrument board standard from here
	54085		Telegauge amended design
	54897		Van with Mulliner temporary facia board
	54906		Body bolt holes pierced in frame
1929 Mar	55506		Ball-type gear change fitted to early cars as follows: Chassis 55506, 55893, 55917, 56080, 56196, 56203, 56229 (car 5TT 28470), 56304, 56490 (car 5TT 28762)
	56519		Ball change standard from here, and rigid luggage grid
May	56203		Starting handle and shaft
	56080		Early cars with finger-tip controls
	57080		Paddle-type shockers
May (third week)			Brake cables and rods. First motion shaft and third speed gearwheel
Jun (first week)			Oil in back axle
Jun	57140; 57251; 58742		Gearbox front cover. Front axle & swivel arms. Rear axle bumpers on frame (apart from 55582)
Aug	59001		Steering finger-tip controls
	59040		Silentbloc shackles
	59402		Steering box cover and worm wheels
	59181-59636	5TF 4451	Low frame intermediate type. All saloons from 59181 have rear tank but special tailpipes
Sep to mid Oct	59502	6T series	Low frame and chrome shock absorber fabric lining
Oct			Brake lining rivets
Mid Nov			Clutch ring and centre. Gearbox rear cover. Third motion shaft and speedo gear
	60900		Wings
Dec	61230		Steering column bracket
	61665		Body brackets riveted to frame Universal joint socket strengthened
1930 Jan			Improved union flange for tank gauge units
	61961		Steering controls with headlamp switch
Feb 10			Grease gun
Feb	62061		Carburettor and air cleaner
	62036		Tank with depression to clear rear axle greasing
	62054		Air cleaner, all from 62061
	62236 (all from 63224)		1930 16/6 type, dash, fan, radiator, starter switch, clutch plate and accelerator controls
Mar	62966		Oil strainer
	(also 62910)		Armstrong shock absorbers on rear axle
	62306		Exhaust downpipe vertical
	63112		R.A. pinion thrust bearing, reverse thread in place of felt
	63194		Hertford on front axle
Apr	63200		Clutch thrust bearing lubricator
	63377		Front wing stay hole ½in further back. (63389-64867 incl.)
	63617		Tail pipe clip removed from tank at rear
	63970		H.F horn
	63955		Different shaft and pinion

Jun	65000		Junction box bracket
	65800		Speedo 80mph
	64416		5.00in by 20in tyres
Aug		6TC 8001	Commence Burnham. RR type
		6TF 2001	Commence fabric KK type
	66468		Steering column loop and switch enclosed
		6TC 8046/6	16/6 fitted with new springs. 12/4 followed a week later
Oct	66930		Side tube swivel arm colonial
Oct 29	66942		Front wings with flanged front edge Steel hinges
Nov	66956		Steering box with accelerator fulcrum cast in
Dec 2			New rear spring fitted to 12/4
Dec 4	67407		Strengthened radiator with overstrap
Dec	67752		First V type carburettor
Dec 30	67721		Aluminium step edging
1931 Jan			Special finish (mot polished) for spring leaves
	68254		Swivel arm
	68347		Radiator support as per 16/6
Apr 22	68473		Front wing
	68537		Cross tube lever and front bumper
	68500		Increased diameter prop shaft
	68592		All black instruments.
Jul 7	68730		Increased bore, different case bush
	68739		First motion shaft and bush
Sep	68758		Taxi high radiator and onwards
Oct	69507		Auster screen with central control mixed – not 69538
Dec			New smaller side lamps
1932 Feb 3	70170		Dynamo
	70391		Headlight dipper switch on steering wheel
May	71001		Hardy Spicer prop shaft
Sep	71601		Thermostat radiator cap
Sep	71814		Luvax shock absorbers
1933 Feb	72351		Twin top gearbox and new brakes
Sep 8	74372		Cross-braced frame; engine rubber mounted; synchromesh on third and fourth gears, except taxi
1934 Feb	75500		Steering column
	76400		Gear change forks
Apr	Eng no 77050 (?)		Oval pistons
Aug	77012		Synchromesh on second gear
	77350		Needle bearing type prop shaft
Oct	77623		Cable operated front brakes
Nov	77817		Cowled radiator, with filler cap under bonnet. Trafficator switch on steering wheel. V-type carburettor. Coil ignition. Foot-operated headlamp dip switch.
1935 Jun 18	79243		Marles Weller steering gear introduced (?)
1936 Feb	80080		Marles Weller (?)
1939 Jul	82015-82778		Also BYO 82106, BYD 82593, 350 to War Department

Summary of models and prices year by year

Date	Model	Price	Notes, reference
1922, Jan	Two-four seater	£550	Catalogue 252
	Touring car	£550	
	All-weather coupé	£675; £695 with leather head	
1922, Sep	Chassis	£380	
	Two-four seater	£450 (standard), £490 (special)	
		By Oct reduced to £440 and £480	
	Tourer	£450 (standard), £490 (special)	
	Harley all-weather coupé	£580; £600 with leather head	
	Berkeley landaulet	£600	
1923, Sep	Chassis	£340	
	Two-four seater	£450 (special)	
	Touring car	£450 (special)	
	Harley all-weather coupé	£525	
	Berkeley landaulet	£525	
	Windsor saloon	£550	
1923, Oct-Nov	Chassis	£300	Catalogue 398
	Two-four seater	£375 (standard), £395 (special)	
	Touring car	£375 (standard), £395 (special)	
	Harley all-weather coupé	£525	
	Berkeley landaulet	£525	
	Windsor saloon	£550	
1925 model year	Chassis	£270	Catalogue 460
	Hertford two-four seater	£355	
	Clifton tourer	£355	
	Harley all-weather coupé	£475	
	Berkeley landaulet	£475	
	Windsor saloon	£475	
1926 model year	Chassis	£245	
	Hertford two-four seater	£350, then reduced to £340	
	Clifton tourer	£350, then reduced to £340	
	Harley all-weather coupé	£425	
	Berkeley landaulet	£425	
	Windsor saloon	£455	
	Iver saloon	£470	With division
1926, Mar-May	Chassis	£245	Catalogue 510 C
	Hertford two-four seater	£315	
	Clifton tourer	£295	
	Harley coupé	£425 (by 1 March)	Not listed by May
	Berkeley landaulet	£425 (by 1 March)	Not listed by May
	Windsor saloon	£395	
	Iver saloon	£405	With division
1927 model year	Chassis	£225	Catalogue 561
	Clifton tourer	£275	
	Open Road tourer	£325	
	Windsor saloon	£350	
	Iver saloon	-	With division
1928 model year	Chassis	£195	Catalogue 600
	Clifton tourer	£255; £260 with Triplex glass	
	Open Road tourer	£295; £300 with Triplex glass	
	Two-four seater	£295; £300 with Triplex glass	No name
	Six-light fabric saloon	£325; £355 with Triplex glass	By April 1928
	Windsor saloon	£325; £355 with Triplex glass	
	Iver saloon	£335; £365 with Triplex glass	With division
	10cwt box van	£325	
1928, Aug	Chassis	£185	

	Clifton tourer	£245; £250 with Triplex glass	
	Open Road tourer	£265; £270 with Triplex glass	
	Two-four seater	£265; £270 with Triplex glass	No name
	Six-light fabric saloon	£315; £345 with Triplex glass	
	Burnham saloon	£315; £345 with Triplex glass	
	Iver saloon	£325; £350 with Triplex glass	With division
1928, Oct	Chassis	£185	Catalogue 655
	Clifton tourer	£245; Triplex screen standard	
	Open Road tourer	£265; Triplex screen standard	
	Special two-four seater	£265; Triplex screen standard	
	Four-light fabric saloon	£305; £325 with Triplex all round	
	Six-light fabric saloon	£315; £340 with Triplex all round	
	Burnham saloon	£315; £340 with Triplex all round	
	Iver saloon	£325; £350 with Triplex all round	With division
1929, Mar-May	Chassis	£187 10s	Catalogue 655 C to F
	Clifton tourer	£250; Triplex screen standard	
	Open Road tourer	£270; Triplex screen standard	
	Special two-four seater	£270; Triplex screen standard	
	Four-light fabric saloon	£310; £330 with Triplex all round	
	Six-light fabric saloon	£320; £345 with Triplex all round	
	Burnham saloon	£320; £345 with Triplex all round	
	Iver saloon	£330; £355 with Triplex all round	With division
1930 model year	Chassis	£187 10s	Catalogue 700 B to D
	Clifton tourer	£250	To about Jun
	Two-seater	£255	No name
	Special two-four seater	£270	Not listed by Mar
	Open Road tourer	£270	Not listed by Mar
	Watford fabric saloon	£275	From about Apr
	Four-light fabric saloon	£310; £320 with sliding sunroof	
	Six-light fabric saloon	£320; £330 with sliding sunroof	
	Sportsman's saloon	£320; £330 with sliding sunroof	
	Burnham saloon	£320; £330 with sliding sunroof	
	Iver saloon	£330	With division
1931 model year	Chassis	£185	Catalogue 764
	Eton two-seater	£275	
	New Open Road tourer	£275	
	Watford fabric saloon	£275; £285 with sliding sunroof	
	Marlow fabric saloon	£299; £309 with sliding sunroof	
	Wycombe fabric saloon	£299; £309 with sliding sunroof	
	Burnham saloon	£299; £309 with sliding sunroof	
	Iver saloon	£309	With division
1932 model year	Chassis	£185	Catalogue 846
	New Windsor saloon	£268	Pressed steel body
	Burnham saloon	£288 incl. sliding sunroof	De Luxe model
1933 model year	Chassis	Not quoted	Catalogue 930 etc
	Harrow two-seater	£255	
	Open Road tourer	£255	
	Berkeley saloon standard	£265	
	Berkeley saloon De Luxe	£285	
	Iver saloon	£295	With division
	Westminster four-light saloon	£315	
1934 model year	Chassis	£190	Catalogue 1028
	Two-seater	£265; £295 by May 1934	
	Tourer	£265; £295 by May 1934	
	Berkeley saloon fixed head	£275	
	Berkeley saloon	£295	
	Westminster four-light saloon	£325	
	Carlton long wheelbase	£305	

	Iver long wheelbase	£315	With division
1934, Aug-Nov	Chassis, short or long	£190	Catalogue 1171
	Berkeley saloon fixed head	£275	
	Berkeley saloon De Luxe	£295	
	Westminster four-light saloon	£325	
	Carlton long wheelbase	£305; £7 10s extra for occasional seats	
	Iver long wheelbase	£315; £7 10s extra for occasional seats	With division
1935, Jan	Chassis	–	Catalogue 1180 A
	Hertford saloon fixed head	£275	
	Hertford saloon	£295	
	Westminster four-light saloon	£325	
	York long wheelbase	£305	
	Chalfont long wheelbase	£315; £7 10s extra for occasional seats	With division

Note: It would appear that the two-seater and tourer models did continue into the 1935 calendar year in limited production, see the detailed tables of production figures.

Production figures 1922 to 1928

	1922	1923	1924	1925	1926	1927	1928	c/f
Chassis	51	255	400	450	750	750	641	3297
Tourer (Clifton)	809	1481	2900	5400	6500	8000	3600	28,690
Open Road							69	69
Coupé	305	584	50					939
Two-four seater		50	100	50	50	54	29	333
Landaulet		97	50	50				197
Saloon (Windsor)			550	2500	2750	5000	3947	14,747
Fabric Saloon						200	1564	1764
Saloon (Burnham)							117	117
Gordon Saloon							429	429
Gordon 2-4 seater							2	2
Mulliner Saloon							1326	1326
Mulliner 2-4 seater							544	544
Hoyal Saloon							40	40
Startin							16	16
Morgan Fabric							2	2
Mulliner Van							1	1
Startin Van							3	3
Other Styles							14	14
Exports							1345	1345
	1165	2467	4050	8450	10,050	14,004	13,689	53,875

Notes: These figures are based on the research by Bob Wyatt undertaken in the 1960s when there were still detailed records at Longbridge.

1) The two-four seater was marketed under different names for almost every year of production. Much of the difficulty arose because the sales staff disliked and often refused to recognise the names they were given by Herbert Austin.
2) Figures for 1922 are to 31 October. Figures for 1923 are from 1 November 1922 to 31 October 1923.
3) Figures for 1924 are from 1 November 1923 to 31 December 1924 and are approximate.
4) Wyatt says that the Open Road tourer was first produced during w/e 6 October 1928. In fact it was produced from late 1926, but Open Road production before October 1928 may be included with the Clifton.

It is interesting to note that of the three models available with the short-stroke engine made prior to October 1926, say about 24,000 cars, in round figures about 16,000 were tourers and two-seaters, 5000 saloons, 900 coupés, 200 landaulets, and fewer than 2000 were fitted with bodies manufactured by outside firms. This shows the great popularity of the open models at this period and although saloons had been available for two years, they had not yet gained ascendancy over the tourers. This was to follow later and if we look at 1929 for example, we will find only a small percentage of the cars produced had tourer bodies.

APPENDIX

Production Figures 1929 to 1935

	b/f	1929	1930	1931	1932	1933	1934	1935	Total
Chassis	3297	676	699	503	347	914	1193	1184	8813
Tourer (Clifton)	28,690	1431	320						30,441
Open Road tourer	69	550	452	108	33	81	54	8	1355
Coupé	939	2							941
Two-four seater	333	324	64	64	19	24	32	8	868
Landaulet	197								197
Saloon (Windsor)	14,747	3266							18,013
Fabric Saloon	1764	874	344	23					3005
Watford Saloon			679	40					719
Saloon (Burnham)	117		3199	1175	1301				5792
Burnham De Luxe					302				302
New Windsor				194	455	12			661
Berkeley saloon				165	260	177			602
Berkeley De Luxe						541	325		866
Iver Saloon					7	8	11	12	38
Westminster					5	47	36	15	103
Carlton Saloon							51		51
Hertford Saloon								117	117
Hertford De Luxe saloon								493	493
York								85	85
Ambulance					12			3	15
Travellers Brougham				17	9				26
Gordon Saloon	429	305	96	37	27	47	10	8	959
Gordon 2-4 seater	2								2
Mulliner Saloon	1326	215	130	17	1				1689
Mulliner 2-4 seater	544	129							673
Hoyal Saloon	40								40
Startin	16								16
Morgan Fabric	2								2
Mulliner Van	1								1
Startin Van	3	17		5	1			19	45
Other Styles	14	13	34			2	10	1	74
Exports	1345	1252	612	117	70	60	35	7	3498
	53,875	9054	6629	2767	2547	1913	1757	1960	80,502

Notes:

5) The saloon figure for 1929 is for Windsors and Burnhams combined.
6) The first Carlton was produced on 24 March 1934.
7) The last tourer was produced during w/e 31 August 1935.
8) From 1936 to 1939, 2085 taxi chassis were manufactured.
9) 263 W/D Utility vehicles were produced from June 1940 until October.